AQA Religious Studies A

Judaism: Ethics

GCSE

Kim Hands

Peter Smith

Series editor

Cynthia Bartlett

Published in 2009 by:
Nelson Thornes Ltd
Delta Place
27 Bath Road
CHELTENHAM
GL53 7TH
United Kingdom

10 11 12 13 / 10 9 8 7 6 5 4 3 2

A catalogue record for this book is available from the British Library

ISBN 978 1 4085 0479 6

Cover photograph/illustration by Top Foto/Imageworks

Illustrations by Rupert Besley and Paul McCaffrey (c/o Sylvie Poggio Agency)

Page make-up by Pantek Arts Ltd, Maidstone

Printed in China by 1010 Printing International Ltd

Photo Acknowledgements

Alamy: Eitan Simanor / 6.10B; Israel Images / 6.3B; 6.5A; Jim West / 5.8A; Peter Marshall / 3.9A; PhotoEdit / 4.8D; PhotoStock-Israel / 3.8C; Ruby / 6.2B; Steve Allen / 3.2B; Stephen Markeson / 3.4B; **Ark Religion**: Helene Rogers / 6.2A; Itzhak Genut / 3.10B; **Corbis**: Bettmann / 3.4C; 3.10A; Gyori Antonie / 6.11A **Fotolia**: CO1; 1.1A; 1.4C; 1.5B; CO2; 2.3A; 2.6B; 2.7C; 2.8A; 2.8C; C04; 3.1A; 3.1B; 3.4D; 3.5A; 3.5B; 3.6A; 3.8A; 3.8B; 4.1A; 4.1B; 4.1C; 4.2A; 4.4C; 4.5B; 4.5C; 4.6B; 4.6C; 4.7A; 4.7B; 4.8C; 4.10B; 4.10C; 4.10E; 5.2A; 5.2C; 5.2D; 5.3B; 5.4C; 5.5A; 5.5B; 5.6B; 5.7C; 5.8B; 5.9A; 5.10A; 6.1C; 6.4B; 6.8D; **Getty**: 3.3C; 3.11A; 6.6A; AFP / 2.4A; 2.4B; 3.6B; 3.7D; Time & Life Pictures / 3.7B; **iStockphoto**: 1.2A; 1.2B; 1.3A; 1.3B; 1.3C; 1.4A; 1.5C; 1.6A; 1.6B; 1.7A; 1.7B; 1.8A; 1.8B; 1.10A; 1.12B; 1.13A; 2.1A; 2.6C; 2.7A; 2.7B; 2.9A; 2.10A; 3.3B; 3.5C; 3.7A; 3.9C; CO4; 4.2B; 4.2C; 4.3B; 4.3C; 4.3D; 4.4A; 4.4B; 4.5D; 4.8A; 4.8B; 4.9B; 4.9C; 4.9D; 4.11A; CO5; 5.1A; 5.1C; 5.3A; 5.4A; 5.7A; 5.9B; CO6; 6.1A; 6.1B; 6.3A; 6.4A; 6.6B; 6.7A; 6.7B; 6.8A; 6.8B; 6.8C; 6.9A; 6.10A; **PA Photos**: Doug Peters / EMPICS Entertainment / 2.2B; Fiona Hanson / PA Wire / 2.1B; Sebastian Scheiner / AP / 6.5C; **Peter Smith**: 1.4B; **Rex Features**: 1.9B; Israel Image / 2.9B; Ray Tang / 2.2A; **Topfoto**: UPPA / 5.6A; **World Jewish Relief**: 2.5B.

Text Acknowledgements

Scripture quotations taken from the Holy Bible, New International Version. Copyright © 1978, 1984 by International Bible Society. Used by permission of Hodder & Stoughton, a division of Hodder Headline Ltd. All rights reserved. "NIV" is a registered trademark of International Bible Society. UK trademark number 1448790.

2.3: Table A.19 in World Population Prospects: The 2006 Revision, Highlights © United Nations (Working Paper No. ESA/P/WP.202. 2007) Reprinted with permission.
2.4: Kofi Annan quotation, reprinted with permission from The Times/NI Syndication.
2.6: Paul Anticoni, Chief Executive of WJR, reprinted with kind permission from World Jewish Relief.
2.7: Material reproduced courtesy of Liberal Judaism, the Union of Liberal and Progressive Synagogues, UK.

Contents

Introduction   5

1 Life and death   8

1.1 Judaism and ethics   8

1.2 The Torah and the mitzvoth   10

1.3 Other sources of Jewish ethical teachings   12

1.4 Life and death – an introduction   14

1.5 The purpose and quality of life   16

1.6 Abortion   18

1.7 Euthanasia   20

1.8 Contraception and fertility issues   22

1.9 Artificial insemination   24

1.10 IVF and surrogacy   26

1.11 Bio ethics – genetic engineering   28

1.12 What happens after death?   30

Chapter 1: Assessment guidance   32

2 Wealth and poverty   34

2.1 The principle of righteousness   34

2.2 Jewish ideas about the community and duties within it   36

2.3 Causes of poverty   38

2.4 Emergency and long-term aid   40

2.5 World Jewish Relief – history, principles and work   42

2.6 World Jewish Relief – a case study: Georgia emergency appeal   44

2.7 Jewish communities improving lives in the UK   46

2.8 Tzedaka   48

2.9 Attitudes to money and giving   50

Chapter 2: Assessment guidance   52

3 Conflict and suffering   54

3.1 Purpose of life and justice   54

3.2 Reconciliation and peace   56

3.3 Suffering   58

3.4 Suffering and anti-Semitism   60

3.5 War   62

3.6 Nuclear war and disarmament   64

3.7 Terrorism   66

3.8 Pacifism   68

3.9 Protest   70

3.10 Reconciliation   72

Chapter 3: Assessment guidance   74

4 The environment   76

4.1 Stewardship   76

4.2 Causes of pollution   78

4.3 Consequences of pollution   80

4.4 Conservation   82

4.5 Jewish responses to conservation   84

4.6 Reflections on the environment   86

4.7 Animal rights   88

4.8 Care of animals   90

4.9 Using animals for research   92

4.10 Stewardship conclusions   94

Chapter 4: Assessment guidance   96

5 **Crime and punishment**   98

5.1   Jewish views on the law   98

5.2   The causes and effects of crime   100

5.3   Punishment and forgiveness   102

5.4   Aims of punishment (1) –
      deterrence and reparation   104

5.5   Aims of punishment (2) –
      protection, reformation,
      retribution and vindication   106

5.6   Types of punishment   108

5.7   The impact of punishment   110

5.8   The death penalty
      (capital punishment)   112

5.9   Teachings of the Torah about
      punishment   114

Chapter 5: Assessment guidance   116

6 **Relationships and lifestyle**   118

6.1   Jewish marriage   118

6.2   Divorce   120

6.3   Divorce and remarriage   122

6.4   Human sexuality   124

6.5   The mikveh   126

6.6   Parents and children   128

6.7   Legal drugs (1)   130

6.8   Legal drugs (2)   132

6.9   Illegal drugs   134

6.10 Jewish schools and yeshivot   136

Chapter 6: Assessment guidance   138

Glossary   140

Index   142

Nelson Thornes has worked in partnership with AQA to make sure that this book offers you the best possible support for your GCSE course. All the content has been approved by the senior examining team at AQA, so you can be sure that it gives you just what you need when you are preparing for your exams.

■ How to use this book

This book covers everything you need for your course.

Learning Objectives

At the beginning of each section or topic you'll find a list of Learning Objectives based on the requirements of the specification, so you can make sure you are covering everything you need to know for the exam.

Objectives

Objectives

Objectives

Objectives

First objective.

Second objective.

AQA Examiner's Tips

Don't forget to look at the AQA Examiner's Tips throughout the book to help you with your study and prepare for your exam.

AQA Examiner's tip

Don't forget to look at the AQA Examiner's Tips throughout the book to help you with your study and prepare for your exam.

AQA Examination-style Questions

These offer opportunities to practise doing questions in the style that you can expect in your exam so that you can be fully prepared on the day.

AQA examination questions are reproduced by permission of the Assessment and Qualifications Alliance.

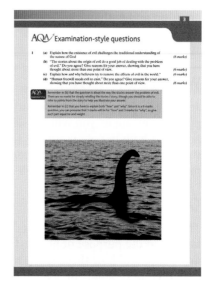

Visit **www.nelsonthornes.com/aqagcse** for more information.

AQA GCSE Judaism: Ethics

This book is written specifically for GCSE students studying the AQA Religious Studies Specification A, *Unit 11 Judaism: Ethics*. You will be studying six very different ethical topics and the Jewish beliefs and teachings that relate to each of these topics. Many of these teachings are from the Tenakh (the Jewish Bible) as it is the main written authority in Judaism. You do not have to be Jewish to be successful but an interest in Religious Studies and a willingness to find out more will help you.

Following this unit alone will earn you a GCSE Short Course qualification in Religious Studies. If you combine it with another unit, you will be eligible for a Full Course GCSE in Religious Studies. In order to qualify for a grade, you will have to sit one 90-minute examination for each unit you study, that is for Short Course, one examination and for Full Course, two examinations. This is the only form of final assessment.

■ Topics in this unit

In the examination, you will be asked to answer questions based on the following six topics.

Life and death

Issues you will study will include fertility issues, contraception, surrogacy, genetic engineering, abortion and euthanasia. The main Jewish teachings about the sanctity of life and life after death are studied in relation to the issues raised.

Wealth and poverty

Jewish teachings give Jews a duty to care for the poor. In this topic, you will consider how this is achieved both in poor countries throughout the world and also in Britain. Attitudes to the use of money, charity and kindness will also be studied.

Conflict and suffering

This topic includes an understanding of the Jewish beliefs on the purpose of life, justice, reconciliation and peace and how these relate to the concepts of suffering, anti-Semitism, war, and protest.

The environment

This includes such issues as pollution, conservation and animal rights and how beliefs about stewardship and the value of the natural world influence Jewish thinking.

Crime and punishment

You will be studying what punishment aims to achieve, types of punishment that can be used along with their impact, attitudes towards the death penalty and how ideas of law, punishment, justice and forgiveness relate to these issues.

Relationships and lifestyle

In this topic, you will consider how Jewish beliefs about law, commitment and responsibility influence attitudes to marriage, divorce and the family, sexuality, social and illegal drugs, and the role of Jewish schools.

■ Assessment guidance

Your examination will be in two parts.

Part A will have four questions split into shorter parts. You have to answer all of the questions in part A, which will total 48 marks.

Part B will contain two questions. Again, they will be split into smaller parts. As you are required to answer just one of these questions, you will have to choose which one. Each of these questions carry 24 marks, so they are longer than in part A and it is likely that you will have to give more detail in some of your answers.

Every chapter in this book finishes with assessment guidance, using questions similar in style to those in your examination. There is also a summary of what you have learned in the topic, together with a sample answer to one part for you to mark yourself. The large grid on page 7 will help you to do this as well as finding out what you have to do to gain high marks.

Examination questions will test two assessment objectives

AO1	Describe, explain and analyse, using knowledge and understanding.	50%
AO2	Use evidence and reasoned argument to express and evaluate personal responses, informed insights and differing viewpoints.	50%

The examiner will also take into account the quality of your written communication – how clearly you express yourself and how well you communicate your meaning. The grid below also gives you some guidance on the sort of quality examiners expect to see at different levels.

Levels of response mark scheme

Levels	Criteria for AO1	Criteria for AO2	Quality of written communication	Marks
0	Nothing relevant or worthy of credit	An unsupported opinion or no relevant evaluation	The candidate's presentation, spelling, punctuation and grammar seriously obstruct understanding	0 marks
Level 1	Something relevant or worthy of credit	An opinion supported by simple reason	The candidate presents some relevant information in a simple form. The text produced is usually legible. Spelling, punctuation and grammar allow meaning to be derived, although errors are sometimes obstructive	1 mark
Level 2	Elementary knowledge and understanding, e.g. two simple points	An opinion supported by one developed reason or two simple reasons		2 marks
Level 3	Sound knowledge and understanding	An opinion supported by one well developed reason or several simple reasons. **N.B. Candidates who make no religious comment should not achieve more than Level 3**	The candidate presents relevant information in a way which assists with the communication of meaning. The text produced is legible. Spelling, punctuation and grammar are sufficiently accurate not to obscure meaning	3 marks
Level 4	A clear knowledge and understanding with some development	An opinion supported by two developed reasons with reference to religion		4 marks
Level 5	A detailed answer with some analysis, as appropriate	Evidence of reasoned consideration of two different points of view, showing informed insights and knowledge and understanding of religion	The candidate presents relevant information coherently, employing structure and style to render meaning clear. The text produced is legible. Spelling, punctuation and grammar are sufficiently accurate to render meaning clear	5 marks
Level 6	A full and coherent answer showing good analysis, as appropriate	A well-argued response, with evidence of reasoned consideration of two different points of view showing informed insights and ability to apply knowledge and understanding of religion effectively		6 marks

Note: In evaluation answers to questions worth only 3 marks, the first three levels apply. Questions which are marked out of 3 marks do not ask for two views, but reasons for your own opinion.

Successful study of this unit will result in a Short Course GCSE award. Study of one further unit will provide a Full Course GCSE award. Other units in Specification A which may be taken to achieve a Full Course GCSE award are:

- Unit 1 Christianity
- Unit 2 Christianity: Ethics
- Unit 3 Roman Catholicism
- Unit 4 Roman Catholicism: Ethics
- Unit 5 St Mark's Gospel
- Unit 6 St Luke's Gospel
- Unit 7 Philosophy of religion
- Unit 8 Islam
- Unit 9 Islam: Ethics
- Unit 10 Judaism
- Unit 12 Buddhism
- Unit 13 Hinduism
- Unit 14 Sikhism

1.1 Judaism and ethics

■ Judaism

Judaism is one of the oldest religions in the world. It can trace its history back nearly 4,000 years to the time of Abraham although some would say that as its scriptures include the story of how God created the Earth, it goes back to the beginning of human life on earth. Others point to the time of Moses the Lawgiver (around the 13th century BCE) as the origin of Judaism as we know it today, as that is when the Jews were chosen by God and given the law. Whenever it started, Judaism is rooted in the Middle East and became centred on Jerusalem, the capital city of modern Israel. This is where the Jews built their most sacred place of worship – the Temple on Mount Moriah, the place earlier where Abraham nearly sacrificed his son Isaac as a test of obedience given by God (Genesis 22: 1–18). The remains of the outer wall of the Temple Mount, which was nearest the most holy part of the Temple, can be seen in the picture below. It has become a focus for prayer and religious observance, symbolising the very existence of the faith, despite a troubled history.

A *Jews praying by the 'Western Wall' in Jerusalem*

Jews have a strong belief that they have been chosen by God to set an example of how God would like the people of the world to live. This comes from the time of the Exodus when the Hebrews, as they were known then, believed that they were chosen by God to escape from slavery in Egypt under the leadership of Moses. It was at this time that they received the law including the Ten Commandments.

⚭links

For more information on the law and the Ten Commandments, see pages 10–11.

Activities

1 From what you have read now and learned previously, who do you think is the founder of Judaism – Adam, Abraham or Moses? Give reasons for your opinion and be prepared to discuss this with others.

2 Can you think of any other building or part of a building that has become as important to a religion as the Western Wall is to the Jews?

◼ Ethics

The Concise Oxford Dictionary defines the word 'ethics' as:

> ❝ the science of morals in human conduct ... moral principles; rules of conduct. ❞

Ethics is therefore all about what is morally the right and wrong thing to do in any given situation. Even though humans seem to instinctively know whether an action is right or wrong, we all have different ways of refining this in our own code of ethics. This is essential if we are to become a useful member of a civilised society.

However you decide what is ethical (moral) and unethical (immoral), there must be something that you base your decision on. This may be a conscious choice or decision; it may be subconscious – seemingly natural. The fact remains, that unless you act entirely on instinct (which is unlikely), your own ethics have a basis in some principle or teaching. You may decide to act upon the principle of 'don't do any harm to anyone or anything'. This would seem to be perfectly reasonable but does this apply to the punishment of murderers? What happens in a time of war? Should you eat animals? These three questions (and many more) have to be answered in order to develop a code of ethics based on the principle of not harming anyone or anything. Some of the most intelligent people ever to have lived developed their own ethical philosophies a long time ago, based on such things as duty, and pleasure outweighing pain, but their theories seem to have become the subject of academic study rather than a widespread basis for living a good life.

Activities

3 Imagine that you have the principle 'don't do any harm to anyone or anything.' Would this extend to the punishment of murderers? Would you go to war against an enemy? Would you eat meat? Explain your decisions.

4 Is there anything that might make it easier for you to make such decisions?

5 'The study of ethics is a waste of time because we are all individuals and will make individual decisions.' What do you think? Explain your opinion.

Summary

You should now know a little about the origins of Judaism and understand what ethics is about.

AQA Examiner's tip

Some Jews spell God as G_d to recognise the fact that Hebrew, their sacred language, has no vowels. It is also considered disrespectful to write the full word because it could be carelessly treated. You are not expected to do this in your exam, but you may do so if you wish.

Discussion activity

With a partner, discuss how you decide what is the right thing to do in a given situation. Does this always lead to you making the right decision? Be prepared to share your ideas with others in the class.

I think I should do it but on the other hand, maybe it isn't the right thing to do.

B

1.2 The Torah and the mitzvoth

The Jewish Law

For Jews, the principle that underpins their code of ethics (their decisions on right and wrong) is quite simple. They make decisions based on what they believe God wants them to do. In order to be able to do this, they need guidance about what God wants from them. They believe that the Ten Commandments, which are included in the 613 laws (**mitzvoth**) that appear in the **Torah** (the first section of the Tenakh – the Jewish scriptures) provide this guidance. The Torah is therefore the source of their knowledge about what God requires from them.

Objectives

Know and understand the basis of Jewish law.

AQA Examiner's tip

If you know Hebrew terms such as mitzvoth and Tenakh, you can use them in the examination without having to explain what they mean.

The Ten Commandments

The **Ten Commandments** originate from about the 13th century BCE. While the Jews were wandering in the Sinai wilderness in the years that followed their escape from Egypt, it is believed that the commandments were given by God to Moses, representing the Jews, on Mount Sinai. They are still very important to Jews, but when they were first given, they were even more remarkable because they were a great advance on laws that other countries followed at that time. For example, the first of them established straightaway that there was only one God (monotheism) – revolutionary teaching to most non-Jews who at that time worshipped many gods. The next three commandments establish how the Jewish relationship with God

A Jews believe that Moses received the Ten Commandments on Mount Sinai

should be maintained by not making idols of him, by not misusing his name and by reserving one day in every week for rest and worship.

The other six commandments provide basic laws for Jews to follow, prohibiting such things as murder, adultery, theft, lying and jealousy. The relationships in families were intended to be strengthened by such laws. The laws became the foundation of the Jewish law that deals with how God wants Jews to relate to other people.

The following is a simple version of the Ten Commandments. You can find the longer version in Exodus 20:1–17:

1 You shall have no other god before me.
2 You shall not make for your self an idol.
3 You shall not misuse the name of the Lord your God.
4 Remember the Sabbath day by keeping it holy.

Key terms

Mitzvoth: the laws of Judaism.

Torah: the five books of Moses and the first section of the Tenakh – the law.

Ten Commandments: a list of religious and moral rules that were authored by God and given to Moses.

Mishpatim: judgement, laws for which reason is clear.

Chukim: statutes – laws for which no reason is given.

5 Honour your father and mother.

6 You shall not murder.

7 You shall not commit adultery.

8 You shall not steal.

9 You shall not give false testimony against your neighbour.

10 You shall not covet (be jealous of) your neighbour's house … or anything that belongs to your neighbour.

◼ The mishpatim – judgements

(Exodus 21:1 to 24:18)

There was now an agreement that God would be the God of the Jews and in return the Jews would keep God's laws. This agreement was known as the Covenant. Following the Ten Commandments in the book of Exodus are 53 other laws or judgements given by God to Moses. They govern treatment of servants, personal injuries, the protection of property, social responsibility, justice and mercy, Shabbat laws and the celebration of festivals. Having given these judgements (**mishpatim**) to people, Moses confirmed the Covenant in a ceremony in which young bulls were sacrificed and half the blood was sprinkled on an altar that Moses had built, with the rest being sprinkled on the people:

Beliefs and teachings

Moses then took blood, sprinkled it on the people and said, 'This is the blood of the covenant that the Lord has made with you in accordance with all these words'.

Exodus 24:8

B *The Ten Commandments were given to Moses carved on two tablets of stone*

◼ The chukim – statutes

While the judgements in the mishpatim are supported with reasons, the **chukim** are laws (statutes) for which reasons are not given. The purpose of obeying them seems to be to follow the will of God. A good example of this is in Numbers 19:1–10. It concerns the creation of 'water of purification' made by sacrificing a red heifer (young cow that has not had a calf) and sprinkling its ashes in water to use to purify people from sin. The laws of Kashrut (food laws) in Leviticus 11:1– 47 and the prohibition of wearing wool woven with linen (Deuteronomy 22:11) are further examples of chukim. Jews obey many of them (although they don't now sacrifice red heifers) because doing so is the Jewish way.

Summary

You should now know and understand what Jewish law is based on.

The link between the law and ethics

Jews take the Torah together with what is known as the 'Oral Law' now written in the Talmud and Midrash to help form the basis of Jewish ethics. The Oral Law, which Orthodox Jews believe was given to Moses along with the Torah, explains how the commandments in the Torah are to be carried out. In essence, if an action breaks Jewish law, it is unethical and wrong. Whenever a new development comes about that requires an ethical decision about whether it is right or wrong, Jewish scholars will consult the Tenakh before making a decision, which is then respected by other Jews. This covers a huge range of issues, such as whether a certain new food product conforms to the laws of Kashrut and is therefore permissible for Jews to eat, or whether Jews are allowed to benefit from the latest development in a complicated area, such as genetic engineering.

A   *Rabbis consult the Torah when making decisions*

The prophets (Nevi'im) and writings (Ketuvim)

The Torah is the first section of the Tenakh (the Jewish scriptures) outlining the law. In addition to the Torah, and also important in helping Jews to develop their ethical philosophy, are the teachings of the prophets (**Nevi'im**) and the other writings (**Ketuvim**).

The prophets (Nevi'im)

The prophets featured in the Tenakh range from Joshua, who took over from Moses as leader of the Hebrews and took them into the Promised Land in the 13th century BCE, to Malachi, who is thought to have lived in the 5th century BCE. During that time, a lot happened to the Hebrews, once they had settled in the Promised Land. They had become part of various empires including the Assyrians and

Objectives

Understand the link between Jewish law and ethics.

Understand that Jewish ethical teaching comes from the writings and the prophets as well as from the Torah.

Key terms

Nevi'im: the books of prophecy in the Tenakh.

Ketuvim: the books of writings in the Tenakh.

B   *Isaiah is one of the most important prophets in the Nevi'im*

AQA   *Examiner's tip*

If using a quotation, try to include in your answer the book the quotation comes from. There is no need for the chapter and verse.

Babylonians (who took influential Hebrews into exile), won several battles and built two temples. Their observance of their religion varied. At times they went far away from what God expected of them and the main role of many of the prophets was to point out the error of their ways and predict punishments that would befall them if they continued to disobey God. The prophet Hosea wrote:

> **Beliefs and teachings**
>
> There is no faithfulness, no love, no acknowledgement of God in the land. There is only cursing, lying and murder, stealing and adultery; they break all bounds, and bloodshed follows bloodshed.
>
> *Hosea* 4:1–2

After identifying the problem, he made it clear that God would forgive them:

> **Beliefs and teachings**
>
> I will heal their waywardness and love them freely, for my anger has turned away from them.
>
> *Hosea* 14:4

Jews today interpret such writings to help them to live the way that they believe God wants them to. Even though the writings are from around 2,500 years ago, they believe that the nature of God does not change, so modern people can learn from the teachings of the past.

The writings (Ketuvim)

These books contain books of poetry and teaching such as Psalms, and Proverbs, and story books which teach by example such as Job and Esther. Their contribution to Jewish ethics is arguably not as great as that of the Torah and the Nevi'im but they contain some interesting advice:

> **Beliefs and teachings**
>
> A wicked man puts up a bold front, but an upright man gives thought to his ways. There is no wisdom, no insight, no plan that can succeed against the Lord.
>
> *Proverbs* 21:29–30
>
> I stay away from a foolish man, for you will not find knowledge on his lips.
>
> *Proverbs* 14:7

Activity

1 Explain the teachings from Hosea. What do you think that Jews today can learn from this teaching?

C *Babylonian art*

Research activity O⌐

For more teachings like the quotation from Proverbs included here, see Proverbs, chapters 10–31.

Activities

2 Explain in detail how Jews make their ethical decisions.

3 Try to write some wise sayings of your own, similar to ones in Proverbs.

4 'Laws and teachings that are over two thousand years old cannot work today'. What do you think? Explain your opinion.

Summary

You should now know and understand that Jewish ethics is based on the Torah, the prophets and the writings, as well as the Oral Law.

1.4 Life and death – an introduction

Life and death

None of us asked to be born. Our parents chose to allow us to be born, once our mothers discovered they were pregnant. We had no influence in that decision. Having been born, for the first few months we had little say over our lives and what happened to us. We were fed and were expected to sleep when our parents decided it was the right time. We went where we were taken and were brought up in whichever way our parents chose. This may have included membership of a religious faith. If our parents were Jewish, we would have been named and circumcised after eight days (if boys), or our names would have been announced in a synagogue service (if girls) for example, traditionally when a month old but more commonly nowadays, a few days after birth. This decision was made on our behalf.

A *Jewish boys are circumcised when eight days old*

Of course, as people become older and more mature, they can decide for themselves what happens to them and whether they wish to continue to follow the religion to which they were introduced as children. Most Jews do choose to retain their Jewish identity; some are devoutly Jewish, keeping the Jewish laws; others may not always follow their faith as strictly.

Unlike being born, people can influence when they die, although Jewish teaching emphasises strongly that they shouldn't. Directly ending one's own life is forbidden in Jewish teaching. However, doing some things that may shorten life, for example, drinking alcohol and smoking, are not forbidden, although taking illegal drugs is.

The sanctity of life

In Judaism, there is a duty to preserve life. Innocent life cannot be taken and death cannot be allowed to come more quickly than it naturally would. Life is considered in Judaism to be a gift from God, who originally created it and it is therefore sacred. Life is to be respected and maintained at all times. Life does not belong to human beings; it belongs to God. Therefore, humans have no right to do anything that may damage it.

Know that the Lord is God. It is he who made us, and we are his; we are his people, the sheep of his pasture.

Psalm 100:3

The teachings about the **sanctity of life** clearly have a great influence on Jewish thinking and on ethical decisions about life and death. If life belongs to God and not to human beings, logically there should be no circumstances when Jews are permitted to damage or take life, whether their own or the life of other people. Some Jews, however, support executing murderers because the Torah states that this should be done on God's behalf and with his authority (for example, Deuteronomy 17:8–13).

However, as life is very different from what it was like 3,000 years ago, issues about life and death are nowadays not as simple as perhaps they once were.

AQA *Examiner's tip*

Make sure that you use the idea of the sanctity of life when explaining or evaluating the Jewish beliefs about life and death issues.

B *Jews believe that God should decide when people die*

C *Some Jews support the death penalty for murderers*

Activities

1 Explain carefully why ending life early is against Jewish beliefs and teachings. Use the sanctity of life in your explanation.

2 Do you think that life should be preserved wherever possible? Give reasons for your opinion.

3 Explain why decisions about issues of life and death are sometimes more difficult to make than they were 3,000 years ago. Give examples.

Summary

You should now understand the idea of the sanctity of life. You should begin to be able to evaluate issues relating to life and death.

The purpose and quality of life

■ The purpose of life

Religion helps to answer some of the 'ultimate questions' of life. If you were to ask a religious person: 'What is the **purpose of life**?' they are likely to involve God in their answer to the question. If you were to ask the same question to someone without a religious faith, there are many answers you might be given. Some people may struggle to come up with an answer at all.

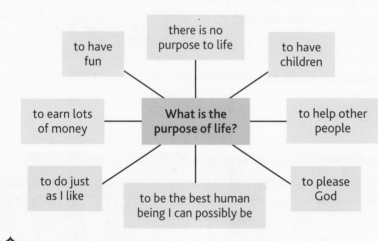

A *What is the purpose of life?*

Of course, you may think of an answer that is not listed in the spidergram. It is likely that a Jewish person would see more to the purpose of life than the answers above. For a Jew, the purpose of life is to serve God and mankind. Serving mankind would involve helping other people, especially those in need. In Jewish thinking, this is why humans were put on the Earth – to serve each other by taking care of the Earth and all it contains, including life, and to serve God by protecting his creation. If enjoyment and wealth result from that then that is good but they shouldn't be the main motivation. The Jewish prayer called the Shema echoes this purpose of serving God.

Beliefs and teachings

Hear, O Israel: The Lord our God, the Lord is one. Love the Lord your God with all your heart and with all your soul and with all your strength. These commandments that I give you today are to be upon your hearts.

Deuteronomy 6:4–6

This is often combined with a verse from Leviticus: *'love your neighbour as yourself'* (Leviticus 19:18), which summarises Commandments 5 to 10, dealing with relationships with other people.

The Jewish belief that this is the purpose of life strongly affects the ethics that Jews develop, relating to life and death.

Objectives

Understand and evaluate Jewish beliefs about the purpose of life and the quality of life.

Key terms

Purpose of life: why a person is alive – what they have to do in their life. The goal of life and the reason for living.

Quality of life: how much a person gets out of their life, a combination of physical and mental factors.

Activity

1 If you had to choose one of the answers to 'What is the purpose of life?' from spidergram A, which one would you choose? Give your reasons. Be prepared to share your answer with others in the class.

AQA *Examiner's tip*

Many people wrongly think that 'love your neighbour as yourself' is one of the Ten Commandments. If you use this teaching, you should refer to it as a summary of the last six commandments, not an actual commandment itself.

The quality of life

In addition to the sanctity and purpose of life, the idea of the **quality of life** is also important. As with the purpose of life, the idea of the quality of life is quite difficult to identify, as it means different things to different people. Put simply, it could be argued that a person's quality of life is good if they are able to fulfil the purpose of life. Thus, if a Jew is able to serve God and mankind, then they have sufficient quality of life. However, for many people, this definition does not work.

Some people interpret 'quality of life' in other terms. Being in good health or having a loving family are seen as being important factors in the quality of someone's life. Having an enjoyable rewarding job also makes a difference. If a person has sufficient money to live comfortably and enjoy their life, their quality of life could be described as good. If they are homeless and have no money, their quality of life could be described as poor. However, nobody would even dream of suggesting that they should give up their right to life because of this! On the contrary, most people would see such a person as someone to help, or someone who needed encouragement so that their quality of life would improve.

A person with a terminal illness who spends most of their time in hospital or a hospice may not feel that they are able to serve God's creation even though they may be able to serve God. They may have a supportive family, but their health is poor and their life is not enjoyable. Their quality of life is likely to be poor but does this mean they should be allowed to die? A Jew would say 'no'.

When considering matters of life and death, Jews take into account the sanctity, purpose and quality of life together, which means that they will invariably seek to preserve life rather than allowing it to be taken away by anybody but God.

B   *Does money give quality of life?*

Summary

You should now understand and have considered how Jewish beliefs affect believers' views about the purpose and quality of life.

C   *Poor quality of life?*

What is an abortion?

Abortion means to remove a foetus from its mother's womb at some time before it is ready to be born. In more than 20 per cent of pregnancies, this happens naturally in the first few weeks of the pregnancy; often before the woman even knows she was pregnant. However, abortion is usually taken to mean a medical procedure in which the foetus is deliberately removed. The use of this 'artificial' type of abortion has aroused much debate for many years, especially from people with religious faith. Some see it as murder of a living being while others interpret it as the removal of just a small cluster of cells which, while having the potential for life, is not alive. If it is true that it is not alive, it cannot be called unlawful killing.

Most people in favour of abortion become more uneasy the longer the pregnancy lasts because the argument that the foetus is not alive becomes more difficult to sustain. British law recognises this by making abortion illegal 24 weeks or more after conception. The decision has to be made by two doctors, who use four criteria in order to make their decision. An abortion is allowed in British law if any of these conditions apply:

1 The pregnancy may risk the life of the mother.
2 The pregnancy may risk the mother's mental or physical health.
3 An additional child will damage the mental or physical health of existing children in the family.
4 There is a serious risk that the child will be born mentally or physically disabled.

The 24-week limit is removed in cases where it is clear that the baby will be born profoundly physically or mentally disabled or if the mother's life or health is severely threatened by the pregnancy.

A

Jewish teaching on abortion

The ideas of the sanctity of life and that humans are created in the image of God (from Genesis 1:27) tend to make Jewish people believe that abortion is wrong. The next verse in Genesis commands people to:

Beliefs and teachings

Be fruitful and increase in number; fill the Earth and subdue it.

Genesis 1:28

While this does not rule out abortion, it does imply that humans should have children and that this is God's will. There is no direct teaching on abortion in the Tenakh, so Jews rely on the Rabbinic interpretation of relevant beliefs and teachings. These tend to focus on the rights of the unborn child against those of the mother. Most believe that until the foetus can survive outside the womb (at approximately 24 weeks provided intense medical care is available), the rights of the mother are more important and abortion is a possibility in some circumstances. The rights of the mother will be the main criteria of whether an abortion should be allowed.

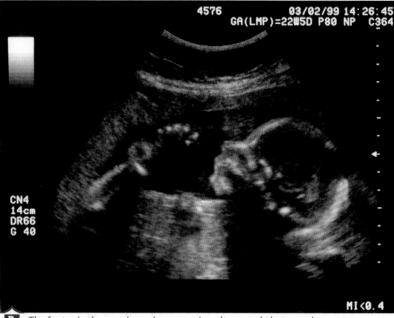

B *The foetus in the womb can be seen using ultrasound photography*

If the pregnancy was a result of rape or incest, or if the baby would be born disabled, abortion is only allowed if the mother can provide sufficient evidence that this will cause her to suffer through ill health or distress. She will take advice and respect the opinion of a rabbi before she decides whether to terminate her pregnancy. If the rabbi shows disapproval, it is likely that she will decide to keep the baby.

In the 11th century CE, Rabbi Shlomo Yitzchaki is recorded as having said:

Beliefs and teachings

As long as it did not come out into the world, it is not called a living thing and it is permissible to take its life in order to save its mother.

Rabbi Shlomo Yitzchaki

The great Jewish philosopher, Moses Maimonides, who lived in the 12th century CE, made it clear that:

Beliefs and teachings

If a pregnant woman's labour becomes life threatening it is permitted to dismember the foetus in her abdomen, either by a medication or by hand.

Moses Maimonides

These two quotations help Jews to decide criteria under which abortion is permitted. Abortion on demand is not a Jewish teaching because Jews see children as gifts of God and believe in respect for all life.

Activities

1 Explain the Jewish attitude to abortion.

2 Do you think that the wellbeing of the mother should be the main criteria for abortion? Give reasons for your opinion.

3 Why do you think a Jewish woman considering abortion is likely to consult a rabbi before making her decision?

Discussion activity

With a partner, try to decide good reasons for abortion. If you don't think there are any, justify your opinion.

Be prepared to share your ideas with others.

Summary

You should now know more about abortion and understand how Jewish beliefs and teachings will influence a Jew's decision to have or not to have an abortion.

AQA Examiner's tip

As abortion is a very personal topic, try to be sensitive when discussing issues arising from it.

A right to die?

The word **euthanasia** means 'a good death'. It is often referred to as 'mercy killing' because its intention is to allow or help a person who is suffering and maybe close to death to die painlessly. The main motivation is **compassion** because by shortening their life by weeks or even days, euthanasia will prevent the person from suffering any further.

In Britain, euthanasia is illegal because it could be seen as assisting someone to take their own life (commit suicide). This is in breach of the Suicide Act 1961. Others believe that people have a right to **self-determination** and that they should be able to control when their own life ends. Euthanasia involves somebody either taking somebody else's life or assisting them to do it for themselves.

There are three types of euthanasia. All are illegal in Britain, but the first two types of euthanasia are performed legally in some countries.

- Voluntary – the doctor ends a person's life at his or her own request.
- Non-voluntary – a doctor consults with relatives to help them to decide whether death is in the sick person's best interest because he or she is too ill to make their own decision.
- Involuntary – a situation in which someone disabled, sick or elderly is killed without consultation for no other reason than they are disabled, sick or elderly.

Objectives

Understand the concept of euthanasia.

Apply Jewish teachings to euthanasia.

Key terms

Euthanasia: inducing a painless death, by agreement and with compassion, to ease suffering. From the Greek, meaning 'Good Death'.

Compassion: a feeling of pity or sympathy that can lead to caring or help.

Self-determination: a person's right to chose what happens to them.

Discussion activities

1 Discuss the picture on this page. Is it a good representation of euthanasia? Explain what you think.

2 Should very ill people have the right to die? Discuss this with a partner. Then write down your thoughts.

A Euthanasia?

If euthanasia is undertaken, it could be passive or active:

- Passive – this is where the dose of pain-killing drugs, such as morphine, is increased, knowing that it is likely to not only control pain but also shorten life. Alternatively, treatment is withheld or withdrawn if all it is doing is delaying the natural process of dying. Some say that this is not really euthanasia at all.

  Withholding treatment to patients who have made it known that they do not want their life to be extended artificially became legal in Israel in June 2006, although it seems to have been done unofficially for many years before that. Now this is done by adding a timer to a respirator which automatically turns off the respirator twelve hours after it sounds an alarm unless the family decide to override it. This means that the machine causes death, and not a person, which would be forbidden.

- Active – giving a drug or deliberately withholding treatment with the sole purpose of causing death.

B   *Jews use a Yahrzeit candle to honour and remember the dead after a funeral*

Jewish teaching on euthanasia

Jewish teachings stress the value of life. For this reason, Jews believe that life should be cherished and respected above everything else except God. Life is sacred; it is provided by God and only he can take it away at a time of his choice. Euthanasia therefore interferes with God's authority. The Talmud makes it clear that euthanasia is killing and therefore against the sixth commandment: 'You shall not murder.'

Beliefs and teachings

One who is in a dying condition is regarded as a living person in all respects.

Talmud – Smachot 1:1

The first case of euthanasia recorded in the Tenakh dates back to around the 13th century BCE when Abimelech, son of Gideon (who ruled over the tribe of Ephraim), commanded his armour bearer to kill him. He chose this death after having been mortally wounded by a woman who dropped a millstone on his head. The book of Judges interprets this as God's punishment on Abimelech.

Activities

2   Explain Jewish teachings about euthanasia.

3   'People who are terminally ill should have the right to choose to end their life early.'

   What do you think? Explain your opinion.

Summary

You should now know what euthanasia is and Jewish attitudes to it.

Activity

1   Make a list of reasons why some people are against euthanasia and why others are in favour of it. Write them down, and add any that a partner has thought of, which you haven't.

Extension activity

Do you think that the Israeli government was correct in making passive euthanasia legal? Spend some time thinking about this and write down your thoughts.

∞ links

For information about the sanctity of life, see pages 14–15.

AQA   Examiner's tip

If writing about euthanasia, try to remember the different types and make it clear whether you are writing about passive or active euthanasia.

Contraception and fertility issues

The choice to have children

The chance for a couple (and increasingly an individual) to choose whether and when they should have children is available to most nowadays. Artificial methods of **contraception** are available for those who choose not to have children but still want to enjoy a full sex life.

However, for Jews, the choice of contraceptives available is restricted. Whilst married Jews are expected to have children in line with the instruction in Genesis 1:28, 'Be fruitful and increase in number' they are allowed to use contraception. Reform and Liberal Jews allow contraception in many circumstances, while Orthodox Jews stipulate just three circumstances:

- if pregnancy or childbirth may harm the mother
- to limit the number of children in a family if this is expected to benefit the family
- to delay having children or space them out.

However, general Jewish teaching restricts the type of contraceptives that can be used. If a contraceptive device damages sperm or stops sperm from reaching their intended destination (for example, a condom), it is not allowed because this is seen as failing to use semen for its intended purpose.

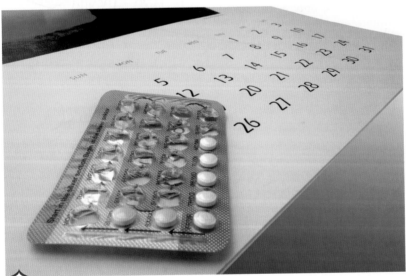

A *Jews are allowed to use contraceptive pills*

Most Jews who use contraception use the contraceptive pill, which is not seen as preventing sperm from reaching its intended destination. This choice is supported by various passages in the Talmud that permit women to drink potions that make them infertile. The health benefits of using a condom to prevent sexually transmitted infection are not of great importance or relevance to Jews personally because they believe that sexual relations should only be shared between a husband and his wife.

Beliefs and teachings

Then Judah said to Onan,"Lie with your (dead) brother's wife and fulfil your duty to her as a brother in law to produce offspring for your brother." But Onan knew that the offspring would not be his; so whenever he lay with his brother's wife, he spilled his semen on the ground to keep from producing offspring for his brother. What he did was wicked in the Lord's sight.

Genesis 38:8–10

In the past, people with fertility problems were unable to be parents. However, today, medical science and technology have provided the opportunity for people to use **fertility treatment** to overcome fertility problems. Some religious people are worried that scientists seem to have taken over from God in deciding who should have children, pointing out that children are a gift from God and not a right.

Modern advances in science are causing problems for believers of any religion because the teachings of their founders and their sacred writings do not refer directly to them. Judaism is no exception. Obviously, when the Tenakh and Talmud were compiled, modern advances in science were unimaginable. Even if God had referred to 21st-century scientific advances when speaking to Abraham, Moses or any of the prophets (which an all-knowing eternal God would be able to do), nobody would have had the knowledge to understand what he was talking about. Consequently, Jewish rabbinic scholars have to identify and interpret their ancient teachings to provide guidance based on general principles, whenever scientists announce a new discovery. The field of fertility issues is a good example of this.

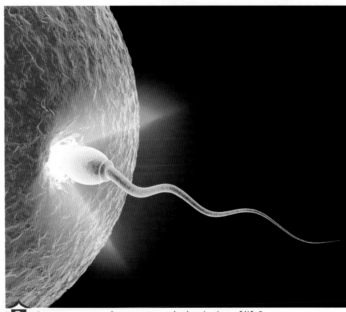

B *A sperm enters a human egg – the beginning of life?*

Summary

You should now know and understand about contraception and fertility issues and Jewish attitudes towards them.

1.9 Artificial insemination

Artificial insemination (AI)

Artificial insemination has been used by farmers for many years as an easy and efficient way of ensuring that animals become pregnant. Without its use, dairy products and meat would be less plentiful and more expensive. Similarly, cross-pollination of plants is a common practice to increase the supply of crops. Few people seem to mind farmers using these processes with animals and plants but some people express concern about the use of similar processes with humans.

A *Babies conceived through AI are sometimes called 'test tube babies'*

When human artificial insemination is used, sperm is collected from a man and inserted into the uterus of a woman via her vagina in the hope that fertilisation will take place and she will become pregnant. There are two types of artificial insemination:

- **Artificial insemination by husband** (AIH) – this is where the sperm comes from the husband of the woman hoping to become pregnant.
- **Artificial insemination by donor** (AID or DI – donor insemination) – sperm is donated (usually for a small fee) by a male volunteer and, after being screened for diseases such as HIV, is used in the same way as in AIH.

Jewish attitudes to artificial insemination

Most Jewish scholars believe that medical advances are authorised by God unless they cause harm. Therefore, because AIH gives life, it is acceptable. However, there is a serious issue about how the semen is collected. Because of the story of Onan (in Genesis 38:8–10), Jews do not allow masturbation.

As there is no artificial way that semen can be produced, this could be a problem. However, some authorities claim that collecting semen for AIH is not causing it to go to waste because it is being used for the creative purpose. Others prefer the husband to wear a condom during intercourse to collect the semen. Because of the rules prohibiting the use of a condom as a contraceptive, if it is used for the purpose of collecting semen, it should have a small hole in it to allow the possibility of conception, however remote this may be.

In cases of AIH, there is no argument about who the father is and conception in this way fulfils the duty to have children. Importantly, any child resulting from this procedure is produced by the two people in a marriage relationship.

However, in AID there is a problem over parentage. While for the donor of the sperm, there is no issue with him following his duty to reproduce, for the 'father' who raises the child there certainly are issues. There could also be problems with inheritance because the laws on the father passing on an inheritance to his children are quite clear and considered to be very important. In the case of a sperm donor, this could become very complex. The resulting child, however, would be Jewish regardless of their father because in Jewish law, if the mother is Jewish, then so is the child. AID makes it possible for single people and female gay couples to become parents. Jews believe this violates traditional family life, which is so important in the faith.

For many Jews, there is also the possibility that a man and a woman who share the same sperm donor father may marry. Even though they are completely unaware that they have the same biological father, their marriage would be classed as incest and therefore sinful.

The main argument against AID, however, is that it can be interpreted as adultery and contrary to the seventh commandment: 'Do not commit adultery' (Exodus 19:14). Thus, it goes completely against concepts of purity and holiness in Jewish family life. In addition, a child conceived through adultery is considered to be illegitimate, losing certain rights in Jewish law.

∞ links

See pages 22–23 for the story of Onan.

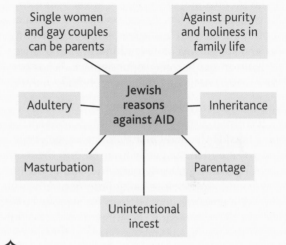

B *Jewish reasons against AID*

Discussion activity

'If a husband and wife both agree to AID because that is the only way they can conceive, it cannot be called adultery.'

Spend 5 minutes discussing this statement with a partner or in a small group.

Activities

3 Write a letter in reply to a Jewish friend who has asked you for advice about whether she should choose artificial insemination because of her difficulty in conceiving naturally.

4 Do you agree with the Jewish beliefs about artificial insemination? If so, explain why. If not, explain why not.

Summary

You should now know and understand more about artificial insemination and have evaluated Jewish attitudes towards it.

C *Louise Brown, born 25 July 1978 – the world's first test-tube baby*

1.10 IVF and surrogacy

In vitro fertilisation (IVF)

The literal meaning of in vitro is 'in glass' to recognise the fact that fertilisation takes place in a glass dish. Children conceived in this way are often nicknamed 'test tube babies'. This technique using human eggs and sperm was pioneered in 1977, and since then, **in vitro fertilisation** has become commonplace. It has helped couples who have no hope of having their own children naturally to become parents.

The procedure involves removing eggs from the body of the mother and fertilising a small number of them with sperm obtained from the father outside the body in a glass dish. One or more of the resulting **embryos** are then medically inserted into the mother in the hope that one will become embedded into the wall of the uterus and begin to develop and grow, before being born naturally around 38 weeks later. Remaining embryos may be deep frozen and stored for future use, possibly, with permission, in embryology or genetic experimentation, or they are destroyed. Success rates for IVF are still quite low and many couples have to undergo treatment several times to achieve success. However, women using IVF are more prone to multiple births. On 26 January 2009, in USA, Nadya Suleman, a single mother through divorce, gave birth to octuplets (eight babies) to add to the six children she already had. All 14 children were conceived through IVF using a friend's sperm. Her case is highly unusual because medical staff would not normally allow so many embryos to be implanted at any one time.

Jewish attitudes to IVF

Although some Jewish scholars reject IVF because they question the validity of fertilising an egg outside the body, most Jews are happy for IVF to take place if doctors believe it is the best remedy for infertility. Indeed, some Orthodox Jews believe that it is obligatory if it is the only way for conception to take place. There are no ethical constraints because they believe that the soul does not enter the embryo until

Key terms

In vitro fertilisation (IVF): a procedure in which eggs are removed from a woman's ovaries and fertilised with sperm in a laboratory. The fertilised egg is then replaced into the woman's uterus.

Embryo: fertilised ovum (egg) at about 12–14 days after conception when implanted into the wall of the womb.

Surrogacy: when a woman agrees to become pregnant and deliver a child for a couple.

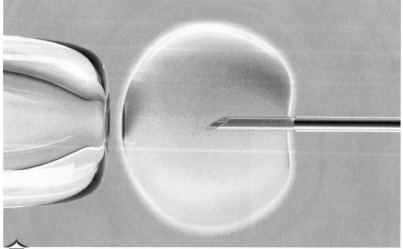

A An egg is fertilised using IVF technology

40 days after conception. They also permit the selective reduction of a multiple pregnancy by aborting one or more embryos if it enhances the possibility of life for the remaining one(s).

However, it is stressed that only the sperm of the husband and the eggs of his wife should be used – there must be no third party donors involved. That way, the sanctity of marriage is maintained and the resulting child is in no doubt about his or her parentage. This can however cause problems with the collection of semen as outlined on pages 24–25.

■ Surrogacy

Fertility treatment can also be used to allow a surrogate mother to conceive. A surrogate mother has a child and then hands it over to a couple to raise as their own child. Normally, the surrogate mother's egg and sperm from the intended father are used via artificial insemination treatment (traditional **surrogacy**). However, if the intended mother has working ovaries, the child can be conceived through IVF, using the mother's egg and the father's sperm, and implanted into the surrogate mother's womb (gestational surrogacy). Once the baby is born, it is handed over to the couple for whom the mother carried it. Under British law, she can be paid expenses but not a fee.

After the child is born, the father will put his name on the birth certificate as the father of the child. This automatically gives him and the surrogate mother equal rights over the child. After six weeks, the couple who intend to raise the child can apply for a parental order. This gives them full parental rights over the child and the surrogate mother loses all the rights she had in the first six weeks. Once the order has been granted, the intended couple receive a new birth certificate with both of their names on, although the old birth certificate is kept and stored by the registering authority.

■ Jewish attitudes to surrogacy

Most Jews are opposed to the idea of surrogacy. Their main argument is that confusion over who the child's mother is affects the religious identity of the child. In Judaism, a child is considered Jewish if they have a Jewish mother, whose role it is to bring the child up within the faith. They are also worried that this can be seen as adultery and there is the potential for incest if the surrogate mother is a family member or if the surrogate child later marries another child born to the same surrogate mother. Some Jews will permit an unmarried Jewish woman unrelated to either the intended father or mother to act as a surrogate, although there are few women who are able and prepared to do this. The fact that she is unmarried and unrelated prevents concerns about adultery and incest (and there could be difficulties in the future) but most Jews still disagree with surrogacy.

Summary

You should now know and understand about IVF and surrogacy and Jewish attitudes towards each. You should also have evaluated issues relating to Jewish attitudes to IVF and surrogacy.

Discussion activity

Discuss with a partner whether IVF should be allowed. Think of two reasons why it should and two reasons why it shouldn't.

After a couple of minutes of discussion, be prepared to share your ideas with the rest of the class. You could then write down the best three reasons for each opinion.

AQA   Examiner's tip

If you are asked in an examination to explain reasons why some people think something, do not use bullet points in your answer, because an explanation needs to have more detail and possibly examples.

∞ links

Find the definition for the term 'surrogate mother' in the Glossary at the back of this book.

Activities

1. Explain what surrogacy is.

2. Do you agree that surrogacy should be allowed? Give your reasons.

3. 'Childless couples should live with the fact that they will never be parents.'

   Do you agree? Give reasons for your answer, showing that you have thought about more than one point of view. Refer to Judaism in your answer.

Over the last 50 years, research into medicine and biology has brought about massive change. Fertility issues are just one field in which these changes have improved the lives of millions of people worldwide. The study of the ethical considerations behind this research and the changes it brings is called **bio-ethics**. One of the most controversial areas of medical and biological research is in the field of genetics. **Genetic engineering** has brought benefits to the human race but some scholars, working in religion and ethics, have expressed doubts and fears over some of the techniques used and some of the potential capabilities that genetic engineering can offer.

I know you can now do this, but have you ever asked yourself whether you should be able to?

A

Objectives

Understand the concept of bio-ethics in the form of genetic engineering in designer babies and saviour siblings.

Apply Jewish ethical teachings to issues about designer babies and saviour siblings.

Key terms

Bio-ethics: the study of ethical dilemmas brought on by the progress and use of science and medical technology.

Genetic engineering: when an animal's or human's genes are modified or manipulated.

Designer babies: babies whose characteristics may be selected by parents to avoid inherited weaknesses or to choose desired physical features.

Saviour siblings: babies selected to provide genetic material for seriously ill relatives.

Genetic engineering

Genetic engineering refers to the modification or changing of the genetic characteristics of a living thing. It can be performed on genes of plants, animals and humans in order to provide benefits for the organism or species. Most of the advances that this research has brought have been of benefit to humans, either directly or indirectly. Genetic modification of crops brings higher yields to provide more food for people and for animals bred for meat. Synthetic insulin, which benefits diabetics, is now produced using modified bacteria and there are hopes that genetic research will in future hold the key to producing a cure for such incurable diseases as AIDS and some forms of cancer.

Human genetic engineering often (but not always) uses human embryos up to 14 days old. This research is strictly controlled, with one of the controls being that embryos must be destroyed no later than 14 days after fertilisation. However there are fears that this technology could be misused.

Discussion activity

With a partner, spend 5 minutes discussing whether there are things that scientists can do that they should not be allowed to do. What are these things and why do you think they shouldn't be allowed to do them? If you think there are none, discuss reasons why you think this.

Designer babies

American scientists have used this technology to produce a genetically modified human embryo. It is now scientifically possible to select genes specifying height, intelligence and hair colour, for example. If allowed, this technology could lead to '**designer babies**', where parents could choose the gender and characteristics they would like their baby to have. While the research is legal, it is currently illegal to use it for the purpose of creating designer babies. There would, of course, be many ethical objections to the research being used in this way. Scientists

∞ links

Look up the meaning of the term 'embryo' on page 26 or in the Glossary at the back of this book.

make it clear that they see the purpose of their work in human genetic engineering as eliminating genetic diseases and being able to screen for healthy embryos for implantation via IVF technology.

Saviour siblings

> **Case study**
>
> ### James and Daniel Cartwright
>
> In the summer of 2004, James Cartwright was born in Cambridge suffering from a rare genetic disease. The only cure for this disease is a transplant of stem cells from a compatible donor. In James' case, the most compatible was judged to be an unborn brother who could be conceived via selective IVF treatment using semen and eggs from James' mother and father. This would allow the doctors to select embryos that did not carry the faulty gene that caused the illness and that were a perfect tissue match with James. Brother Daniel was born in November 2006 and, after his birth, doctors collected stem cells from his umbilical cord. These were then used to cure James.

As in the above case study, it is now possible for doctors to use stem cells collected from the umbilical cord of a sibling to treat some serious genetic illnesses. The child born specifically for this purpose is called a '**saviour sibling**'. This possibility was developed by genetic technology on embryos. However, in law, it is only permitted to create a saviour sibling using stem cells and not organs (for example, kidneys) or other cells or tissues that could cause harm to the donor. A further issue is that unused embryos created for the purpose must be disposed of after, at most, 14 days.

Jewish responses

Most Jews are in favour of genetic engineering if it is used to cure or eliminate disease but opposed to its use in creating designer babies. They believe that God has given mankind a duty to make the world a better place and the knowledge to do so. Eliminating previously incurable diseases would achieve this with few ill effects. If surgery is permitted on people, it should also be permitted on embryos so, they argue, manipulating the genetic make up of an embryo does not cause a problem. Disposing of embryos within the 14-day limit is also permitted because, as they have not been implanted, there are no ethical considerations associated with their disposal because Jews believe they do not have the status of a person at this stage.

There are those who disagree, however, because despite this technology being used to heal, it can be seen as showing a lack of faith in God and as altering his creation.

Summary

You should now know and understand about genetic engineering in relation to designer babies and saviour siblings and Jewish attitudes towards these issues.

Activities

1 Why do you think that some people would prefer to choose their baby's gender and characteristics?

2 If allowed, what would be the three most important characteristics you would choose in a designer baby? Give your reasons. What would be least important? Why?

AQA Examiner's tip

If you are evaluating bio-ethics, you could use designer babies and saviour siblings as examples for two different points of view – designer babies for the 'disagree' argument and saviour siblings for the 'agree' argument perhaps.

Activities

3 Explain what a saviour sibling is.

4 Do you agree that creating and using saviour siblings should be allowed? Explain your reasons.

5 Explain Jewish attitudes towards genetic engineering.

6 In your opinion, are Jews correct in holding these attitudes?

Extension activities

'Any technology that helps people cure currently incurable illnesses has to be good, even if the technology can be misused.'

1 What do you think about this statement? Give reasons for your answer.

2 How do you think a Jew would respond to this quotation? Explain why.

Life after death

Unlike most other religions, there is little teaching in Jewish holy books that explain what happens after death. The emphasis is on correct living, not death. Jews are, however, convinced that death is not the end but would say that they do not know about the details of what it may be like. Despite their uncertainty about what happens after death, Jews use the idea of life after death to help motivate themselves to live in a way they believe that God intends, by worshipping him as a way of showing their love for him, and by following his laws in order to show love for their neighbour – the rest of God's creation.

There are verses in holy books that give bits of information and by putting all these bits together, a more complete picture

I may not be sure what it is like, but I trust God to reward me for all the good I have done.

A

begins to emerge, although there are different interpretations of these passages. For this reason, there is disagreement between Orthodox Jews, who follow Judaism in a strict traditional way and Reform Jews, who are more modern in their interpretation of the Tenakh. Early teachings in the Torah refer to rejoining one's ancestors upon death. The phrase used to describe this is 'gathered to his people'.

Beliefs and teachings

Then he breathed his last and died and he was gathered to his people, old and full of years.

Genesis 35:29

However, over time this belief appeared to change.

Sheol

Sheol is mentioned in several places in the Tenakh, including in the Torah. It is described as a shadowy place of darkness and silence where all souls exist without consciousness. Job seems to be referring to Sheol when he wrote:

Beliefs and teachings

Turn away from me so that I can have a moment's joy before I go to the place of no return, to the land of gloom and deep shadow, to the land of deepest night, of deep shadow and disorder where even the light is like darkness.

Job 10:20–22

In later parts of the Tenakh, the idea that Sheol is a temporary state develops. From this, the idea of **immortality of the soul** arises.

■ Immortality of the soul

This idea means that when the body dies, the soul separates from the body and lives on. Many Jews believe that there are no teachings in the Tenakh to support this view, tracing its origins back to between the 1st century BCE and the 1st century CE. There are some undeveloped teachings about this in the Talmud. However, as belief in the immortality of the soul grew, many Jews, especially from the Reform tradition, included it in their ideas about what happens after death.

■ Resurrection

The belief in **resurrection** is mainly held by Orthodox Jews. The prophet Daniel, whose prophecies were probably written down during the 2nd century BCE long after his death, looks forward to a time of resurrection. This time will mark a reunion of the soul and the body to live again at a point in the future. The righteous would then enjoy their rewards, and the wicked would receive appropriate punishments.

Beliefs and teachings

Multitudes who sleep in the dust of the earth will awake: some to everlasting life, others to shame and everlasting contempt. Those who are wise will shine like the brightness of the heavens, and those who lead many to righteousness, like the stars for ever and ever.

Daniel 12:2–3

The Talmud gives a few further ideas about resurrection but there are many Jews today, mainly from the Reform tradition, who reject resurrection of the dead.

■ Judgement

Reform Jews have no specific official belief about **judgement** and the world to come and there is much debate about who qualifies to go to heaven (Gan Eden) and hell (Gehinnom) and whether these are two states of consciousness or actual physical or spiritual places. The fate of the righteous is not in question but whether *hell* is the permanent resting place for everybody else or whether for some it is only temporary is unclear. Moses Maimonides, the Jewish philosopher from 12th century CE, made it clear that *heaven* is not exclusively for Jews when he wrote:

Beliefs and teachings

'The pious of all nations of the world have a portion in the world to come.'

Moses Maimonides

■ The Messianic age

Some Jews believe in a time in the future when the Messiah will come. At that time, the righteous dead will resurrect and live in a time of peace in a restored Israel.

Activity

1   Do you think image B is a good representation of judgement and heaven? Explain your reasons.

B   *A representation of judgement and heaven?*

Activities

2   Write a sentence about each of the six sections on these pages to show the beliefs of the Jews related to life after death.

3   Choose one of the four quotations on these pages. Explain what it tells you about Jewish beliefs.

4   How do you think that believing in life after death affects the everyday life of a typical Jewish person? Give examples.

Summary

You should now know and understand different opinions in Judaism about life after death and have evaluated how these beliefs may affect behaviour.

1

Life and death – summary

For the examination you should now be able to:

✔ explain how the Jewish ideas of the purpose of life and quality of life influences attitudes to:

 – the sanctity of life

 – abortion and euthanasia

 – fertility issues – contraception, in vitro fertilisation (IVF), artificial insemination by the husband (AIH) or donor (AID or DI)

 – surrogacy

 – bio-ethics – genetic engineering in designer babies and saviour siblings

 – beliefs in the immortality of the soul, resurrection and judgement

✔ apply relevant Jewish teachings to each topic

✔ discuss topics from different points of view, including Jewish points of view.

Sample answer

1 Write an answer to the following exam question.

 'Describe Jewish beliefs about abortion.'

 (6 marks)

2 Read the following sample answer.

> Jews believe that God created human beings and told them to increase in number (Genesis). Therefore no Jewish woman should be allowed to have an abortion. However, some Jews think abortions are OK especially if the health of the mother is at risk. I think this is just an excuse to disobey their religion. The Jews say the health of the mother is more important than her baby but I think the health of the baby is just as important.

3 With a partner, discuss the sample answer. Do you think that there are other things that the student could have included in the answer?

4 What mark would you give this answer out of six? Look at the mark scheme in the Introduction on page 7 (AO1). What are the reasons for the mark you have given?

Examination-style questions

1   Look at the photograph below and answer the following questions.

(a) Explain why some Jews might be against surrogacy?   (*4 marks*)

 As there are four marks available, try to give and explain at least two reasons with some specific Jewish teaching.

(b) Give two reasons why a Jew may be in favour of artificial insemination by husband (AIH).   (*4 marks*)

 If you are asked to give two reasons and four marks are available, you will earn two marks for each of two reasons (provided they are correct and each one given is explained clearly).

(c) 'If a couple cannot have a child, they should just accept it.'
     Do you agree? Give reasons for your answer, showing that you have thought about more than one point of view. Refer to Judaism in your answer.   (*6 marks*)

 Before you start writing, think carefully. You have to provide reasons, including reasons taken from Jewish beliefs for each of two different points of view and explain how they relate to the quotation.

2.1 The principle of righteousness

Righteousness

As the word implies, **righteousness** is all about doing what is right. It means behaving in a just and fair way – a way that happens to be promoted by Judaism along with other faiths. Putting the interests of other people alongside our own and acting in a way that is right for all are important elements in righteousness. Actions that exploit or harm others are not. Kindness is an act of righteousness because it leads to an action that is right.

Righteousness in the Tenakh

The book of Genesis tells a fascinating story of the saving of one righteous man and his family who were saved from the destructive power of God when he removed corruption and violence from the earth:

> **Beliefs and teachings**
>
> Noah was a righteous man, blameless among the people of his time, and he walked with God ... Now the earth was corrupt in God's sight and was full of violence. God saw how corrupt the earth had become, for all the people on earth had corrupted their ways. So God said to Noah, 'I am going to put an end to all people, for the earth is filled with violence because of them.'
>
> *Genesis* 6:9–13

Whatever you make of the story, it was perhaps written as an attempt to show that righteousness is pleasing to God, whereas corruption and violence are not. Those who live righteously will receive a reward; those who don't, will not.

In the 8th century BCE, while looking forward to the day of the Lord, the prophet Amos emphasised that righteousness is pleasing to God when he said:

> **Beliefs and teachings**
>
> Let justice roll on like a river, righteousness like a never-failing stream.
>
> *Amos* 5:24

The place of righteousness in wealth and poverty

It is a fact that the world contains many people who are wealthy, many more who are poor, and a large number in between. Many countries are, for various reasons, poor while others are rich. Some see this inequality to be in conflict with righteousness.

A *Noah survived the flood because he was a righteous man*

Jews live all over the world. Some live in poor countries but the majority live in wealthy countries. Israel, the Jewish homeland, where around 75 per cent of the population is Jewish, is a country whose economy places it within the top 25 per cent of countries in the world.

The six countries with the largest Jewish populations, accounting for around 90 per cent of the world's Jews (USA, Israel, France, Canada, Britain and Russia), are all wealthy, economically developed countries. Despite this, Jews are keen to help those who are less fortunate than themselves.

Righteousness in today's society

Righteousness is a difficult word to find a Hebrew equivalent for. Many believe that the closest Hebrew word is 'tzedek'. However, Rabbi Jonathan Sacks (Chief Rabbi of the United Hebrew Congregations of the Commonwealth) defines tzedek as:

> 66 *Justice, charity, righteousness, integrity, equity, fairness and innocence* (which he goes on to summarise as) *justice with compassion.* 99
> *(from Covenant and Conversation: Thought on the weekly Parsha from the Chief Rabbi.*
> *13 August 2005)*

In a similar way to the prophet Amos, in Rabbi Sacks' eyes, righteousness and justice go together as qualities that God wants to see within individuals and their communities.

This seems to be a good way of thinking when trying to define exactly what righteousness means. So a 'righteous' person today might be one who possesses all or many of these qualities.

Righteousness was praised at the time of Noah and the prophet Amos (among others) also saw that it was a much needed quality. These thoughts are echoed by Rabbi Jonathan Sacks today, so it should be very clear what God expects from Jews. They should always act righteously towards others within society. This includes those who are suffering from the effects of poverty, whether in Israel, Britain or anywhere else throughout the world.

links

For reasons why some countries are poor, see pages 38–39.

Activity

1   Do you think it is harder to help those less fortunate than yourself if you live in a wealthy country? Give reasons for your opinion.

AQA   Examiner's tip

If you can remember quotations from present-day Jewish people, you can use them to develop your answers.

Activities

2   Explain fully what you think the word 'righteousness' means to a Jew.

3   What do you think 'God expects Jews to live righteously towards one another' means? Give some examples of what they may do to achieve this.

Summary

You should now understand the meaning of righteousness and have begun to evaluate its place in matters of wealth and poverty.

B *Rabbi Jonathan Sacks speaks on behalf of Jews in Britain and the rest of the Commonwealth*

Jewish ideas about the community and duties within it

The community

The Talmud tells a story of Rabbi Hillel, who lived in the 1st century CE. A non-Jew challenged him to teach him the whole of the Torah in the length of time he was able to stand on one foot. If he succeeded, the non-Jew would convert to being Jewish. The great rabbi replied:

Beliefs and teachings

What is hateful to yourself, do not do to your fellow man. That is the whole Torah; the rest is just commentary. Go and study it.

Rabbi Hillel

In other words, Rabbi Hillel was offering a summary of the Torah that gave the essence of Jewish ethical teaching based on Leviticus 19:18: 'love your neighbour as yourself'. The command to study the Torah emphasises how important it is in everyday life to show love to everybody within the community whether Jew or Gentile. Furthermore, the Mishnah (an ancient book of Rabbinic writings) teaches that the world is based on three things: the law, service to God and loving kindness. That is what lies behind the 613 mitzvoth in the Torah and it is what informs the Jewish beliefs about the community and their obligations (what they should do) and duties (what they must do) within it.

Family

The most immediate community is the family. In Judaism, the family is very important, as reflected in the fifth commandment:

Beliefs and teachings

Honour your father and mother.

Exodus 20:12

The home is central for Jews. For many centuries, Jews have been persecuted for being Jewish and public worship and keeping the faith was often difficult or impossible. The home gives them the security and trust that they need.

Jews are obliged to marry fellow Jews and have a duty to have children, who should be brought up within the faith of their parents. This ensures that a married couple support and encourage each other and their children in the expectation that they will remain as members of the Jewish faith. This gives the children a sense of identity and security because they are brought up in the faith of their parents and are likely to have Jewish friends who have the same beliefs and observe the same practices.

Business

Many Jews have become business people (for example, Roman Abramovich, Sir Philip Green and Sir Alan Sugar) taking note of the Jewish law's teachings on fair business practices. False weights and

Objectives

Understand Jewish ideas about the community.

Analyse how these ideas are interpreted in Jewish ethics today.

Activities

1   Do you think that Rabbi Hillel's response was a good one? Explain your reasons.

2   Is 'love your neighbour as yourself' a good ethical basis for living? Explain your reasons.

3   What obligations and duties do you think that Jews have to their community?

A *Sir Alan Sugar, prominent Jewish businessman*

measures are forbidden, buying and selling must be ethical, that is, a fair price should be paid for a fair product or service. There should be no exploitation of either buyer or seller and wages should be paid in full and on time. These are all considered duties required by their faith. Thus, Jews obeying these laws and recognising their duties make good and trusted business people and employers, to the benefit of the local, national and global communities they serve.

These ethical teachings, focussed on love, kindness, honesty and fairness, should be used in everyday life to benefit both the individual and the community in which they live.

Discussion activity

With a partner, discuss how 'love your neighbour as yourself' may help a business person to become successful.

Esther Rantzen

Esther Rantzen has become one of the best-known and most loved Jewish women in Britain. She was one of the most recognised celebrities on television between 1973 and 1994 through writing, producing and presenting the popular weekend television programme *That's Life*. It was a mix of serious consumer stories, light-hearted items and good news stories that at the height of its popularity was watched by well over 10 million people every week.

In 1986, arising out of her desire to help the most vulnerable members of the community, she produced and presented a programme called *Childwatch*. This alerted the British public to shocking issues of child abuse, poverty and suffering. One development that came from this was Childline, a freephone service that allowed distressed children to call a helpline. In the first 48 hours after opening, Childline was swamped with calls mainly about sexual abuse that victims had been unable to talk about to anyone before. Originally, Childline was planned to be a temporary facility for young people but it soon became clear that it needed to exist permanently. Esther Rantzen managed to obtain sponsorship and funding, premises and a freephone number from BT. The permanent Childline was born.

B *Esther Rantzen, founder of Childline*

Childline now has 12 bases around the UK and because of the huge demand for the service, has merged with the NSPCC (National Society for the Prevention of Cruelty to Children) to ensure that Childline continues. In 2008, they reported counselling 13,237 child victims of sexual abuse who had contacted Childline, an increase of more than 50 per cent over the figure for 2005.

Although Childline is not a specifically Jewish organisation, it was founded by a prominent Jewish woman who was able to use her contacts within the community to help her to finance and launch the charity.

Research activity

Find out more about Childline at www.childline.org.uk

Activity

4 Note down some details about Childline.

Esther Rantzen, along with other Jewish people involved in working for the good of the community, does not necessarily claim a religious motivation for her work. However, her upbringing and adherence to the faith provides a lasting influence for good and inspires her social conscience to follow the instruction in Leviticus 19:18 – 'love your neighbour as yourself.'

AQA Examiner's tip

If you use Childline as an example of an organisation that helps the community, make sure that you mention that it was founded by Esther Rantzen, a well-known Jewish woman.

Summary

You should now understand more about Jewish obligations and duties in the community and be able to use an example in your writing.

2.3 Causes of poverty

Introduction

One of the biggest problems faced by many people in the world is poverty. At least a quarter of the world's population do not have sufficient food, lack clean drinking water and have little access to healthcare for themselves or their children. While there are numerous reasons why this situation exists, we will look at the main four.

Climate

Much of the continent of Africa has a climate that is very hot and dry, especially in the countries across the north of the continent. This makes it very difficult for farmers to grow crops and rear animals to feed their families. More importantly, such drought conditions mean there is insufficient water for people to drink and because the countries are poor, they are not able to collect and keep the water that falls during the rainy season for when it is needed. Indeed, in some years, there is no rainy season.

Global warming is making matters worse. Climate change is resulting in the dry regions becoming drier and the wet regions becoming wetter. This trend is likely to continue, resulting in millions of people facing the real prospect of starvation, unless rich countries provide them with food. To make matters worse, climate change is a result of global warming, which is mainly being caused by the actions of wealthy countries rather than poor ones and yet it is the poorer countries who are suffering the most.

Population growth

Another cause of poverty is population growth, especially in countries that can least afford extra mouths to feed. In most rich countries, roughly as many babies are born as people die. However, in poor countries, the lack of contraception means that the population is increasing. In addition, with the possibility of babies dying in infancy, people are likely to have more children to ensure that they have someone to contribute to the family and care for them in later life.

B

Country	Number of live births per thousand that die by their fifth birthday
Mali	199.7
Somalia	192.8
Chad	189.0
The World	73.7
United Kingdom	6.0

Objectives

Understand and evaluate four causes of poverty.

Discussion activity

Spend two minutes thinking carefully about what it must be like living without sufficient food, water and healthcare. Discuss your thoughts with a partner.

A *In some poor countries, water has to be collected and carried home*

Activity

1 Write a short passage to express how the figures in Table B make you feel.

AQA Examiner's tip

You will not be expected to quote figures, but it will help if you show that you know that there are big differences between countries.

Economic reasons

The system that governs what countries buy and sell to each other and the price they are able to charge does nothing to help most inhabitants of poorer countries. Producers of crops like wheat and rice sell their crops to the country that pays the most for them and not to needy countries who cannot afford them. As a result, poorer countries have to depend on what they can produce themselves. In addition, some wealthy farmers use valuable agricultural land to grow cash crops such as fruit, flowers and vegetables that they can sell to rich countries, keeping the profit for themselves. This does not benefit local people because the money does not get shared out with them.

Research activity

Find Saudi Arabia and Yemen on a world map to find their location in relation to the UK and other parts of the world.

Location and resources

A country's geographical location can determine its wealth. This is partially due to its climate but also whether it has natural resources like oil and minerals that richer countries want to buy. Countries in the Middle East have a climate that is very hot and dry – the sort of climate that would normally lead to poverty. However, because some of them have large reserves of oil within their boundaries, they are very wealthy while others without oil are extremely poor. Saudi Arabia has 25 per cent of the world's oil so far discovered and, in common with many countries around the Persian Gulf that have oil to sell, is therefore very wealthy despite its hot dry, climate.

However, Yemen is a country bordering Saudi Arabia where the situation is rather different. The people in Yemen produce less oil and their reserves of oil and gas are much less than those in Saudi Arabia. So Yemen is a poor country, despite sharing a border with a rich one.

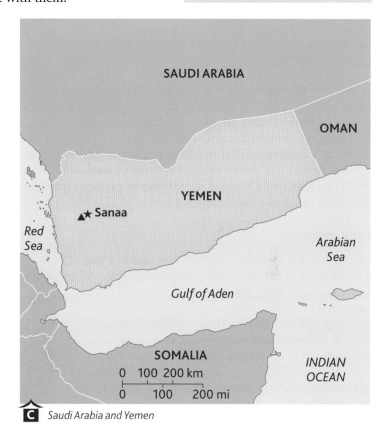

C   Saudi Arabia and Yemen

The average life expectancy in Yemen is 59 for men and 63 for women, while in Saudi Arabia it is 71 for men and 75 for women.

Activities

2   Note down the **four** causes of poverty described on these pages. Who or what is to blame for them?

3   Which of these causes do you think is the one that is likely to cause most poverty? Give your reasons.

4   Which causes least poverty? Explain your answer.

Extension activity

Try to think of or find out some other causes of poverty. Note them down and give a brief explanation.

Summary

You should now understand four causes of poverty and have evaluated their effect.

Emergency and long-term aid

Two types of aid

Every religion (together with many non-religious organisations) has set up voluntary agencies to respond to areas of the world where there are people suffering from the effects of poverty, or from a natural disaster. In this way, they allow their ethical beliefs, which are inspired by their faith, to be shown through their actions.

Emergency aid

Emergency aid has to be provided immediately after a disaster occurs. Delays in offering help can cost the lives of those who initially survived the disaster but perhaps suffocate in collapsed buildings or die from the injuries they sustain because there is no one to help them when they need it most. The immediate requirement is for food, water, medical supplies, shelter, clothing and search teams to look for survivors. Transport is essential, not only to get relief workers to where they are needed, but to take casualties to nearby hospitals and other survivors to a place of safety. However, many natural disasters make this impossible because such things as earthquakes, floods and volcanoes can make roads impassable.

Long-term aid

Once the initial response has been met and as many lives as possible are saved, **long-term aid** takes over from emergency aid. Its role is to rebuild the destroyed buildings, villages and towns so that the residents can eventually return. This can take years but it is essential. It is acknowledged that the best people to do this work are local people with the required skills. They need building materials and in some cases advice and management to provide an overall solution, but many are able to contribute to the rebuilding process – indeed, such rebuilding provides necessary labour and gives survivors a sense of purpose and hope. Other sorts of long-term aid include training, project funding, and so on.

Both types of aid are necessary if communities are to be able to resume their normal way of life as quickly as possible.

Objectives

Understand the difference between emergency and long-term aid.

Analyse the types of aid given to the victims of the Kashmir earthquake in 2005.

Key terms

Emergency aid: giving needy people short-term aid as a response to a crisis or disaster, e.g. food in times of famine or war.

Long-term aid: helping needy people to help themselves by providing the tools, education and funding for projects. This type of aid is given by World Jewish Relief.

A *A woman looks at the wreckage of her home after the Bangladesh cyclone 15 November 2007*

Activity

1 Write 8 tasks connected with emergency aid. Draw a symbol to represent each task.

The Kashmir earthquake 2005

On 8 October 2005, the region of Kashmir in Northern Pakistan was shaken by a massive 7.6 magnitude earthquake. The damage was immense, with towns and villages near the epicentre of the earthquake being totally destroyed. Emergency aid was quickly organised but there were delays reaching some of the worst affected areas due to the roads being destroyed, bad weather, landslides and the mountainous terrain. Two weeks after the earthquake, The United Nations Secretary General Kofi Annan called for an:

'immediate and exceptional escalation of the global relief effort ... a second, massive wave of death will happen if we do not step up our efforts now. I expect results. There are no excuses. If we are to show ourselves worthy of calling ourselves members of humankind, we must rise to this challenge.'

(www.timesonline.co.uk)

Kofi Annan was referring to an estimated 120,000 survivors, many of whom had injuries, who had not been reached by rescue teams. In all, nearly 80,000 people died as a result of this earthquake and over 100,000 were injured including many who had to have limbs amputated just to remove them from collapsed buildings.

Twelve months on from the disaster, work on rebuilding was slow. The government of Pakistan gave compensation to people whose houses needed to be rebuilt but many complained that it was not enough to rebuild their homes to the earthquake-resistant standards that the government insisted upon. Relief agencies were still active but unable to meet the massive rebuilding costs especially as the earthquake had been replaced in the international news by other events and funding specifically given for the work had dried up. Families were dreading having to spend another winter in a temporary shelter.

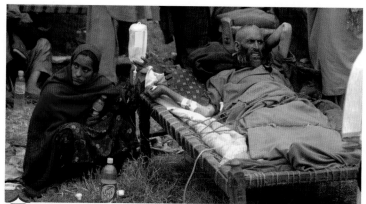

B *Three days after the earthquake, volunteers set up a basic clinic in the ruined town of Balakot*

One of the many organisations involved in helping the victims of the Kashmir earthquake was World Jewish Aid. In a statement, a spokesperson, recognising the need for both emergency and long-term aid, said:

66 *WJAID will initially be assisting with the emergency and then focusing longer term on helping the victims to rebuild their lives and livelihoods. Immediate aid is required to provide the survivors with basic supplies of water, food, medicines, clothes and shelter. It is important that there is a Jewish response to this disaster – it is our responsibility to show what a positive part we, as Jews, play in the world as a whole.* 99

www.worldjewishaid.org.uk

Research activity

For more information about the Kashmir earthquake, do a search at **news.bbc.co.uk**

Activities

2 Using the Kashmir earthquake as an example, carefully explain the difference between emergency aid and long-term aid.

3 Write a diary entry for a relief worker trying to reach survivors in the mountainous region of Kashmir. Think about the anger and frustration you must have been feeling because you couldn't reach the people who needed your help.

AQA Examiner's tip

If you are writing about relief workers offering aid, try to make it clear whether you are referring to emergency aid or long-term aid.

Summary

You should now understand the difference between emergency aid and long-term aid, and the types of help that can be given by organisations.

World Jewish Relief – history, principles and work

History

World Jewish Relief (WJR) has become the main overseas aid charity responding on behalf of the UK Jewish community to both Jewish and non-Jewish needs and emergencies. However, it started life with a different name and with a different purpose.

In 1933, an organisation called 'The Central British Fund for German Jewry' (CBF) was started with the intention of taking Jews out of Germany and allowing them to settle in other countries, mainly in Britain where they would be safe. This is because they feared the rise of Hitler in Germany and were concerned for the safety of Jews living within Germany. Between 1933 and 1939, they helped around 70,000 Jews to leave Germany and settle in safer countries.

On 9 and 10 November 1938, on a night that has become known as Kristallnacht (the night of broken glass), violence broke out in Germany and Austria against the Jewish population. Several were murdered, many were beaten and synagogues were set alight. Homes and businesses were destroyed and 25,000 Jewish men were rounded up and taken to concentration camps, where they were treated shamefully. On 12 November top Nazis, including Hermann Göring and Joseph Goebbels, met to discuss the economic impact of the damage and to decide on further measures to be taken against the Jews. SS leader Reinhard Heydrich reported 7,500 businesses were destroyed, 267 synagogues had been set alight (with 177 totally destroyed) and 91 Jews were killed. Three weeks after this event, 10,000 Jewish children were brought to England from Germany by CBF – a move that almost certainly saved their lives.

A *A synagogue burns in Ober Ramstadt, Germany, 9 November 1938*

Once the Second World War was over in 1945, CBF were involved in helping Jewish communities around the globe come to terms with what had happened during the war, helping Jewish refugees in Britain and bringing orphaned child survivors of the war from central Europe to Britain.

As the need for support after the war reduced, CBF changed its focus to helping Jews in need of support throughout the world. In 1968, they assisted in the evacuation of 4,000 Jews from Czechoslovakia after the Soviet invasion. To recognise their increasingly global focus, in 1978, CBF changed its name to World Jewish Relief (WJR) and has continued to offer support and practical help to Jewish communities that need them.

World Jewish Relief today

Today, WJR is the leading international agency responding to the needs of Jewish communities throughout the world. At times of need, they also work to help non-Jews, providing a channel for the charitable donations of British Jews to be distributed wherever they are required.

Their mission statement is:

> 66 *The relief and assistance of persons in circumstances of need including (but not limited to) Jewish refugees or any other Jewish persons and the relief of sickness and physical disability in any part of the world in such manner and on such terms and conditions (if any) as may be thought fit.* 99
>
> *Mission statement, World Jewish Relief*

In other words, their purpose is to help people in need, especially but not exclusively Jews, wherever they are in the world. The work of the organisation is based firmly on Jewish ethical teachings, the main one being 'love your neighbour as yourself' in Leviticus 19:18. The prophet Micah made it clear to people in the 8th century BCE that God requires his people:

Beliefs and teachings

To act justly and to love mercy and to walk humbly with your God.

Micah 6:8

That is what WJR aim to do.

In this way, WJR show their commitment to the whole world community and to the demands of their faith. Their sensitivity to suffering and need may be heightened by the fact that the Jews themselves have faced terrible suffering, most notably in the Holocaust during the Second World War.

> 66 *World Jewish Relief still faces many difficult challenges but every day we reach out and touch even more lives.* 99
>
> *www.wjr.org.uk*

 World Jewish Relief logo

Research activity

Find out more about World Jewish Relief at www.wjr.org.uk

Discussion activity

Anne Frank, a young victim of the Nazis in the Holocaust, is quoted by World Jewish Relief: 'How wonderful it is that nobody needs to wait a single moment before starting to improve the world.'

With a partner, work out what Anne Frank was trying to say. How much evidence can you see of people starting to improve the world?

Extension activity

How greatly do you think the aims of World Jewish Relief have been influenced by its beginnings as the Central British Fund for German Jewry?

Activities

1. Briefly outline the history of World Jewish Relief from its days as the 'Central British Fund for German Jewry' to the present day.

2. Explain how Micah 6:8 can be used to influence people's behaviour today?

3. What do you think the difficult challenges that WJR face are? Explain your choice.

Summary

You should now understand more about the history, principles and work of World Jewish Relief.

World Jewish Relief – a case study: Georgia emergency appeal

Background

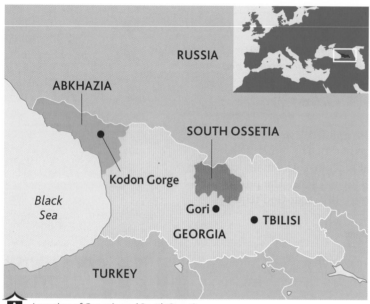

A Location of Georgia and South Ossetia

Objectives

Gain further knowledge and understanding of the work of World Jewish Relief by looking at a case study.

⚭ links

For more information about World Jewish Relief see pages 42–43.

B The national flag of Georgia

South Ossetia is a region in Georgia where the majority of the population appears to support breaking away from Georgia and forming a separate independent state. They have been allowed to run their own affairs since 1992 but Georgia has denied them their wish for independence. Their larger and more powerful neighbours, Russia, support South Ossetia and have recognised their independence.

In August 2008, the issue came to the attention of the world, when Georgian troops moved into South Ossetia with an aerial bombardment and land attack against people whom they saw as rebels. Russia responded by sending its own troops to South Ossetia to defend Russian citizens living there and their own peacekeepers who were already there. Georgia defended its actions by saying that they realised the Russians were moving into South Ossetia anyway so they were just defending their own territory.

Russian troops then moved into Georgia itself, occupying territory including the strategically important town of Gori which is on the main road linking Eastern and Western Georgia. They stopped short of Tbilisi, the capital of Georgia, before pulling their troops back from Georgia to South Ossetia after a ceasefire had been negotiated.

People caught up in the conflict were forced to flee, some into Russia, while others fled to other parts of South Ossetia and Georgia including Tbilisi.

Discussion activity 👥

With a partner, discuss what emotions you would feel if you were forced to flee your home because you were in fear of your life. Who would you look to stay with? Explain why.

The World Jewish Relief response

There has been a Jewish presence in Georgia for around 2,600 years. There are currently around 10,000 Jewish people living there, many of whom were innocently caught up in the conflict and had to flee their homes in fear of their lives. World Jewish Relief (WJR) quickly identified over 700 vulnerable Jews (the elderly and children) whom they believed were in need of support. Many of the 700 had been part of a WJR support programme for two years before the conflict. Some of the people who fled were being housed by fellow Jews in Tbilisi.

Paul Anticoni, Chief Executive of WJR commented:

> 66 *The outbreak of violence has caused extreme distress, and has necessitated huge upheaval for many. WJR is proud to be in a position to call on the Jewish Community to help us to support those who have been affected by the situation.*
>
> *WJR is working with a trusted local partner on the ground to channel effectively the funds raised and ensure as many people as possible, particularly those most at risk, are protected.* 99
>
> Paul Anticoni

Activities

1. Explain how WJR responded to the conflict.
2. Why do you think the Jews seem to be more concerned in helping fellow Jews rather than everyone?
3. Do you think that the reasons you have given in question 2 are good reasons? Explain why/why not.

Two weeks after the conflict ended, the Georgian government encouraged displaced people to return home. However, many of the people from Gori were unable to return to their own homes because of the damage the conflict had caused. They were provided with temporary accommodation including tents, schools and kindergartens (schools for very young children). It was expected that this support would be needed for around six months, that is, through the winter. In addition, food shortages and huge increases in gas prices made their already disrupted lives more difficult.

WJR again became involved in ensuring that displaced people were able to survive the winter by funding partner organisations already working there alongside their own aid workers. This made their response more effective because relief workers already in the country had a better knowledge and understanding of where aid was most needed than aid workers coming in from outside. Help was given both to displaced people and those who had been able to return to their homes to ensure that their basic needs, for example, food and power were provided for. As a result, displaced people were eventually able to return to their homes and rebuild their lives with the continuing support of WJR. People who had been able to return home were supported in their attempts to get back to the way of life they were used to.

WJR pledged that it would continue to support the people of Georgia for as long as needed and keep working with the vulnerable, with whom they had previously worked with since well before the conflict.

C   *The city of Gori*

Extension activity

Write a letter from a person helped by WJR in Georgia thanking them for what they have done. Include some indication of what they have done to help you.

Summary

You should now be able to use a case study to show an increase in your knowledge and understanding of the work of WJR.

2.7 Jewish communities improving lives in the UK

Introduction

While it is very easy to understand the desire of any religion to do all they can to assist people all over the world who are suffering from the effects of poverty, believers also recognise that they should not forget those who are closer to home. Even though people in Britain do not often suffer from the terrible natural disasters or armed conflict described earlier in this chapter (unless family members and friends are in the armed services fighting overseas), there are a significant number of people in Britain who are in urgent need of support. One branch of Judaism that has a strong focus on giving such support is Liberal Judaism.

Liberal Judaism

Liberal Judaism describes itself as the 'dynamic cutting edge of modern Judaism'. It tries to preserve the traditions that are important in the faith but recognises that modern pressures in the lives of individual Jews and their families and communities may need a different approach to solving them. Liberal Jews see themselves as 'the Judaism of the past in the process of becoming the Judaism of the future.' (**www.liberaljudaism.org**).

Liberal Jews account for around 8 per cent of Jews in Britain but in September 2008, together with leaders from Reform and Masorti Jews, they signed a declaration calling for openness, tolerance, collaboration, and respect between these Jewish groups, which represent about a third of all British Jews:

> Diversity is a reality within the British Jewish community but true pluralism (treating with respect other groups and their philosophies) is not, yet. We believe that British Jewry both needs and deserves better.
>
> news.reformjudaism.org.uk

The credit crunch – the Pe'ah fund

In 2008, the banking and economic systems in Britain and elsewhere in the world suffered severe difficulties. Governments worldwide have spent hundreds of billions of pounds supporting the banks in the face of overwhelming losses. In effect, some of the banks had become technically bankrupt. Banks had lent money to individuals and companies who were unable to afford the repayments on their loans. Consequently, the banks ran short of money meaning they could not lend money to each other so were unable to give their clients the support they

A There are many people in Britain who are in need of support

needed. This became known as the 'credit crunch'. Businesses large and small struggled and some ceased trading, for example, Woolworths and MFI, and this increased the number of people unemployed.

As part of their response to the credit crunch, Liberal Jews were encouraged to give 1 per cent of their annual salaries to a fund called the Pe'ah fund to help individuals or groups hit hardest by the credit crunch and unable to access other financial support. They took their inspiration from Leviticus 19:9–10:

Beliefs and teachings

When you reap the harvest of your land, do not reap to the very edges (pe'ah) of your field or gather the gleanings of your harvest. Do not go over your vineyard a second time or pick up the grapes that have fallen. Leave them for the poor.

Leviticus 19:9–10

Rabbi Pete Tobias summed up the reasoning behind the appeal:

66 *We live in a society that is becoming increasingly fragmented and isolating people from each other. Our everyday lives are dominated by material needs. Perhaps it's time to consider what really matters to us as individuals, as families, as communities and recognise that by offering support and encouragement to each other we can bring comfort and hope into all of our lives.* 99

Material reproduced courtesy of Liberal Judaism, the Union of Liberal and Progressive Synagogues, UK

This example is typical of many others that are improving lives right across Britain. Many wealthy Jewish people whether Orthodox, Reform or Liberal provide a lot of money to establish Jewish community centres, schools, advice centres and facilities within synagogues. This may include providing funding to support a rabbi who not only leads worship but also works within the community. Rabbis visit the sick, comfort the dying and their families, and provide counselling to those in need. They also get involved in community, administrative, and educational activities. They may not directly help those suffering from poverty but their acts of kindness do provide facilities that are open to the whole Jewish community and others who feel they may benefit from them.

B   *Many high street stores closed as a result of the credit crunch*

C   *We have ourselves, our family and our faith. What more can any of us need?*

Summary

You should now know and understand about Jewish communities in the UK that attempt to relieve poverty and suffering.

Introduction

Since the 1st century BCE, Jews have not made offerings to God in the form of sacrifices. Before that date, animal sacrifice and offerings of crops were widespread as was tithing (giving 10 per cent of their income to the poor). Nowadays, giving help to other people can be seen as taking the place of sacrifices because Jews are still required to give 10 per cent of their income (after tax has been deducted) as a tithe.

In Jewish tradition, people who need to accept help from others, do the person giving the help a favour, because giving to the needy pleases God.

What is tzedaka?

A simple definition of **tzedaka** is charity. However, in the case of tzedaka, a simple definition is not really sufficient. Charity suggests generosity on the part of the giver as they give to the poor. How much or little is given in charity is entirely down to the individual. However many believe that the amount given should be meaningful to the giver. Donating £20 to charity will have no meaningful effect on the life and finances of a millionaire – a student doing the same is more likely to notice the effect on their life because it is likely they will have to go without something they want or need.

The true meaning of tzedaka is giving to the poor as an act of kindness, justice, righteousness and duty. It is not an option but compulsory, and Jews understand that they will gain spiritual rewards by this giving. Along with repentance, and prayer, tzedaka is one of the three actions that taken together will gain forgiveness from God.

Some Jews see tzedaka as a debt. It is money they owe to the poor. Indeed, if they don't give it, they are robbing the most vulnerable members of society of resources to which they have a right.

Objectives

Know and understand about tzedaka.

Evaluate the importance of tzedaka.

Key terms

Tzedaka: doing righteous acts, giving to charity.

AQA   Examiner's tip

Tzedaka can also be spelt Tzedakah. Whichever way you spell it in the exam will be acceptable.

A   *An orthodox Jewish man begging for money*

prayer   repentance

God's forgiveness

tzedaka

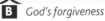

B   *God's forgiveness*

How much is tzedaka?

The law on tithing tells Jews that they are required to give 10 per cent of their income in tzedaka. This has been interpreted to be 10 per cent of what is left over after taxes have been deducted. However, if giving tzedaka makes a person a burden on society because they do not have sufficient money left over to live, they can reduce the amount they give in tzedaka. The money is usually given to organisations that support the poor, healthcare organisations and educational establishments. This is believed to be better than just handing money to a poor individual, which can be interpreted as humiliating to the recipient, and a better way of supporting not just fellow Jews but non-Jews (Gentiles) as well. The 10 per cent is not to be seen as a maximum amount to give; voluntary donations should also be given as an act of kindness when needed.

Jewish teaching makes it clear that a person should not rely on tzedaka but should try to ensure that they take work offered to them no matter what it is. However, nobody should be too proud or ashamed to accept tzedaka because refusing it would be equivalent to making yourself suffer.

The Talmud describes different levels of tzedaka which the 12th century Jewish philosopher Moses Maimonedes put into a list. According to him, the eight levels are:

1 giving begrudgingly
2 giving less than you should, but giving it cheerfully
3 giving after being asked
4 giving before being asked
5 giving when you do not know the recipient's identity, but the recipient knows your identity
6 giving when you know the recipient's identity, but the recipient doesn't know your identity
7 giving when neither party knows the other's identity
8 enabling the recipient to become self-reliant.

The further down the list you go, the better the type of giving is believed to be.

links

See pages 34–35 for more on righteousness and justice.

See pages 34–35 for more on righteousness and justice.

Discussion activity

With a partner, discuss whether you feel it is better for charity giving to be compulsory or voluntary. Think of reasons for your opinion and also reasons somebody may give for disagreeing with you.

Activity

1 Do you think that seeing tzedaka as a debt to the poor is a helpful way of looking at it? Give your reasons.

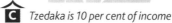

C Tzedaka is 10 per cent of income

Activities

2 Explain carefully what tzedaka is.
3 Add two more levels to Moses Maimonedes' eight levels and place them where you think they should appear on the list.
4 'Nobody should be too proud or ashamed to accept tzedaka.' What do you think? Explain your opinion.

Summary

You should now know and understand the concept of tzedaka and have evaluated its importance.

Health and work

Jews see wealth as a blessing from God. However, they warn against putting too much focus on accumulating wealth at the expense of their family, community and religious duty.

Beliefs and teachings

When you have eaten and are satisfied, praise the Lord your God for the good land he has given you. Be careful that you do not forget the Lord your God, failing to observe his commands, his laws and his decrees... Otherwise when you eat and are satisfied ... and your silver and gold increase and all you have is multiplied, then your heart will become proud and you will forget the Lord your God.

Deuteronomy 8:10–14

The fourth commandment about the Sabbath day, guards against this and reminds Jews of their responsibilities to God.

A wealthy person has a clear responsibility to use their wealth for the benefit of their family and also the wider community. Greed in accumulating money, which can lead to selfishness in using it, is often considered to be worse than poverty.

Money should be earned from working because laziness is frowned upon and gambling is discouraged although not forbidden. Proverbs refers to the importance of the proper use of time and the need not to waste time.

Beliefs and teachings

Remember the Sabbath day by keeping it holy. Six days you shall labour and do all your work, but the seventh day is a Sabbath to the Lord your God.

Exodus 20:8–10

AQA Examiner's tip

You do not have to know quotations off by heart, you can paraphrase them. Do not use quotation marks if you are paraphrasing.

Beliefs and teachings

How long will you lie there, you sluggard?

When will you get up from your sleep?

A little sleep, a little slumber, a little folding of the hands to rest –

and poverty will come on you like a bandit

and scarcity like an armed man.

Proverbs 6:9–11

Wealth then is to be earned honestly and will be based on work. So it is seen as a blessing, but at the same time carrying a responsibility to others. This is an important teaching for Jews, some of whom have earned considerable wealth in business. Judaism therefore considers that it is perfectly acceptable for people to be wealthy provided that:

- their business is run *ethically*, that is …
- their wealth is used for the *benefit of others*, and not just themselves,
- *God is not overlooked* and
- they pay their full amount of *tzedaka* while also making voluntary donations to people and organisations in need including the synagogue.

A   *A wealthy family light a menorah candle, showing their commitment to the faith*

Pushkes

One of the responsibilities of Jewish parents is to bring their children up with knowledge and understanding of their faith. Part of this is done in practical ways by involving the whole family in their religious observances. Many Jewish homes have a pushke. This is a collecting box for putting in money for a charitable purpose. All members of the family, including children, are encouraged to use it because it encourages kindness, which is viewed as a positive quality. Children may put small items of loose change into a pushke or, to emphasise the importance of giving, their parents may give them money to put into the pushke for them. It is considered good manners for guests to put an anonymous contribution into the pushke if they feel they want to.

Pushkes may be for a particular cause such as World Jewish Relief, Childline, the local synagogue or hospital or they may take the form of a more general collecting box and the money divided between several causes. They encourage regular giving as a normal part of everyday life rather than making contributions infrequently. The intention is that the pushke should further the spirit of righteousness both in the home and in the community. Involving children in this is an excellent way of encouraging and developing their faith and Jewish lifestyle.

Activities

5   Explain what a pushke is.

6   Why do Jews believe that pushkes are an important feature of family life? Try to think of at least three reasons.

7   'Everybody should have a pushke in their home.' Do you agree? Give reasons and explain your answer, showing that you have thought about more than one point of view. Refer to Judaism in your answer.

Summary

You should now understand how Jewish attitudes to money encourage giving and be able to evaluate Jewish practices and attitudes to wealth.

Activities

1   Choose **one** of the three quotations on these two pages. Think carefully about it and explain fully what it means.

2   Using the italicised words and phrases in the bulleted list, place the **four** conditions in your own order of importance. Put the one that you feel is most important first. Explain your choice of the most and least important.

3   Compare your list and reasons with a partner's list and reasons.

4   'A wealthy person should use their wealth for the good of others.' What do you think? Explain your opinion.

B   *A pushke*

Discussion activity

With a partner, spend a couple of minutes discussing whether you think Jewish children should be expected to put their own money into a pushke.

Discuss some reasons that people who disagree with your opinion may give to support what they think.

2

Wealth and poverty – summary

For the examination, you should now be able to:

✓ explain the Jewish ideas of righteousness and the concept of community and relate them to:

- what causes poverty

- types of aid – emergency and long-term

- the work of Jewish relief organisations and agencies in world development and the relief of poverty

- the work of World Jewish Relief and the principles on which this work is based

- the work of Jewish communities in UK to relieve poverty and suffering

- the practice of tzedaka

- kindness

✓ apply relevant Jewish teachings to each topic

✓ give your own opinions about each topic and discuss different points of view including Jewish ones.

Sample answer

1 Write an answer to the following exam question:

'Tzedaka is the most important part of Jewish life.'

Do you agree? Give reasons and explain your answer, showing you have thought about more than one point of view.

(6 marks)

2 Read the following sample answer.

> Jews believe that tzedaka, prayer and repentance are the three ways to obtain God's forgiveness. That would seem to suggest that all three are the most important parts of Judaism. However, in my opinion, the statement is true. Tzedaka is all about other people. Jews have to show kindness to each other and what better way is there of being kind than to help people who need help? Tzedeka is not just about money though. It is about acting righteously to other people and God wants people to be righteous – prophet Amos looked forward to a time when righteousness would 'flow like a river'. However, some Jews would say that obeying the 10 commandments is the most important part but I disagree because tzedaka is more important than the law.

3 With a partner, discuss the sample answer. Do you think that there are other things that the student could have included in the answer?

4 What mark would you give this answer out of six? Look at the mark scheme in the Introduction on page 7 (AO2). What are your reasons for the mark you have given?

AQA Examination-style questions

1   Look at the photograph below and answer the following questions.

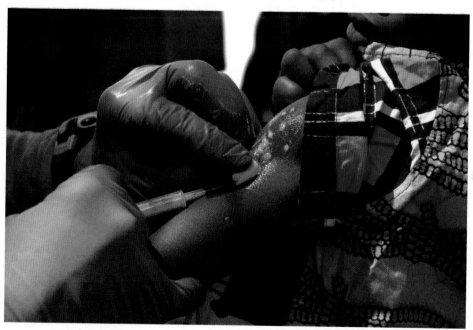

(a) (i) Name a Jewish organisation that helps the poor.   *(1 mark)*
        (ii) Briefly describe the work of the organisation you have chosen.   *(3 marks)*

AQA Examiner's tip Because the question asks you to name an organisation, you will not earn the full four marks if you don't name one.

(b)   Explain briefly **two** causes of poverty.   *(4 marks)*

AQA Examiner's tip An example for each cause will probably help you explain it better although this is not essential to earn full marks.

(c)   'Jews should do more to help the poor.'
          Do you agree? Give reasons for your answer, showing that you have thought
          about more than one point of view. Refer to Judaism in your answer.   *(6 marks)*

AQA Examiner's tip It is important when answering questions of this type that your written communication should be accurate.

3 Conflict and suffering

3.1 Purpose of life and justice

■ Introduction

This chapter looks at Jewish views on conflict and suffering. It examines how Jewish teaching about the purpose of life, justice, reconciliation and peace influences Jewish attitudes. It explores how these teachings are related to war, peace and protest and how Jews today respond to these issues.

The purpose of life

In Judaism, the Torah provides an essential guide to life. It explains the relationship between God and man and it is this that underlines the **purpose of life** for all Jews and demands complete obedience to God's will. In the creation story, people were created by God to have dominion and control over the world. God has entrusted people with the responsibility of using, developing and managing his creation. Therefore, part of the purpose of life for all Jews is the stewardship of the natural world and everything created within it.

The Torah teaches that humans are unique in creation because they have the ability to think and reason. God gave people the gift of freewill, which means that people are able to make decisions and choices for themselves. Every individual has the ability to strive and achieve knowledge and understanding of their relationship with their creator. True happiness and contentment in life can only be realised with the appreciation that there is a higher intellect and that complete commitment to God is the ideal.

For Jews, the purpose of life is to serve God and fulfil God's will for them as explained in the Torah. The mitzvoth (laws) provide a guide to living correctly. They include commandments for worship, family life and conduct in society. Life on earth is a preparation for the world to come. It is therefore important to use this life to develop spiritually. Actions both good and bad will be judged in the afterlife and the soul must be cleansed before it can receive any divine reward. Studying the Torah and keeping the mitzvoth are the only ways to achieve perfection of the soul and to fulfil the divine purpose of life on earth.

> ### Beliefs and teachings
>
> Fill the earth and subdue it. Rule over the fish of the sea and the birds of the air and over every living creature that moves on the ground.
>
> *Genesis* 1:28
>
> Now all has been heard; here is the conclusion of the matter: Fear God and keep his commandments, for this is the whole duty of man.
>
> *Ecclesiastes* 12:13

Objectives

Understand Jewish views on the purpose of life and justice.

A *The Torah guides Jews in their daily lives*

Key terms

Purpose of life: the goal of life and the reason for living.

Justice: bringing about what is right, fair, according to the law or making up for a wrong that has been committed.

∞ links

Read more about the creation story on pages 76–77.

Extension activity

In small groups, discuss what you believe to be the main purposes of life on earth. Use some of the ideas to create a collage illustrating the purpose of life. Use newspaper cuttings, clip art or draw your ideas.

∞ links

Look back at Chapter 1 for more on the Torah and the mitzvoth.

Justice

Justice can be described as 'right and fair actions based on just laws'. In the *Ethics of the Fathers* (Jewish sacred writings) truth, justice and peace are described as the pillars of the world. Justice can only be achieved in the presence of truth and peace. For Jews, achieving these ideals is a sacred duty. In *Jeremiah*, practising justice through righteousness and care of the poor is a way to know God. Establishing justice in the world is therefore the only way to bring about harmony and peace between all people.

God has given people the responsibility for bringing about justice in the world. The Torah and the prophets have been sent by God to help mankind understand and achieve justice. The mitzvoth provide guidance not only on legal justice, but also on the fair treatment of the poor, women, gentiles and others. Jews are expected to act against injustice and make things right between people. It is considered to be wrong to ignore injustice and the suffering of others.

Achieving justice is very difficult and Judaism recognises that there needs to be a balance between the rights of individuals and society. In the treatment of criminals, for example, justice can only be achieved where there is also compassion and mercy. The Midrash (a collection of writings that explain the Tenakh) explains how God chose to create a world with both justice and mercy in order that it might last.

Creating just and fair societies needs every individual to contribute. Jews believe that they must live their lives correctly following the laws of the Torah; if they do this it will help to create harmony in society. Outside of Israel, Jews also take an active part in the governing of society. Many Jewish people work in government, law, education, and so on. This is one way to be active in the development and implementation of justice.

Summary

You should now know and understand Jewish beliefs about the purpose of life and the concept of justice.

B *Achieving Justice in law and society is a sacred duty for Jews*

Living in peace

'Shalom', meaning peace, is the usual greeting offered by Jewish people. Creating a world in which truth, justice and peace are present is a responsibility Jews believe that God has entrusted to people. In the book of Genesis, God gave human beings the gift of conscience and freewill. Unlike other animals, humans have the capacity to choose the right actions for themselves. God provided guidance through the Torah and the prophets, to enable people to know him and his will for them.

Throughout the Jewish scriptures, there are laws and guidance on how to establish a peaceful society. Jews believe that by following God's commandments, peace and justice can be created. The most important teachings are summed up in the Ten Commandments. These include rules for worship and for correct moral living. Another important set of laws is the Noahide Code, revealed to Noah following the great flood that destroyed all life because of people's increasing wickedness. The statements in the Noahide Code sum up the minimum needs to establish a moral and spiritual life.

It is not always easy to know right and wrong today. There are many new issues not discussed in sacred writings because such issues had not arisen then. However, Judaism teaches that God gave people the intelligence and reason to find the correct moral path. People should be guided by their conscience to do the right thing, when there is no law to follow. Jews believe that when people act in a good way, they improve themselves and become closer to God.

Reconciliation

It is inevitable that sometimes people disagree. Human nature is such that there will often be differences of opinion and people have to compromise and work together in order to create harmony. Judaism teaches the importance of finding ways to promote goodwill between people and that people need to find peaceful ways to reconcile differences.

Objectives

Understand Jewish views about reconciliation and peace.

Beliefs and teachings

He has shown all you people what is good. And what does the LORD require of you? To act justly and to love mercy and to walk humbly with your God.

Micah 6:8

THE NOAHIDE CODE
WORSHIP ONLY ONE GOD
DO NOT BLASPHEME
DO NOT MURDER
DO NOT STEAL
DO NOT COMMIT SEXUAL MISCONDUCT
MAKE LAW AND ORDER SO PEOPLE
MAY LIVE IN PEACE

TEN COMMANDMENTS
1 HAVE NO OTHER GODS BEFORE ME
2 DO NOT MAKE IDOLS
3 DO NOT BLASPHEME
4 KEEP THE SABBATH DAY HOLY
5 HONOUR YOUR FATHER AND MOTHER
6 DO NOT MURDER
7 DO NOT COMMIT ADULTERY
8 DO NOT STEAL
9 DO NOT BEAR FALSE WITNESS
10 DO NOT BE JEALOUS OF OTHERS BELONGINGS

A *Jewish law codes*

Extension activities

1 In what ways are these two law codes different?
2 Which do you think is the best code for a community to live by? Explain your answer.

Reconciliation means bringing an end to disagreements and establishing friendly relationships. This means that the people involved have to accept that they have done wrong and be prepared to change. Sometimes, those wronged have to be prepared to forgive those who have wronged them. Only when both parties are prepared to listen and compromise can reconciliation be made. The state of being reconciled is one of harmony and peace.

B *The United Nations works for peace and reconciliation around the world*

Jacob and Esau (Genesis 25–33)

Jacob and Esau were the sons of Isaac. When Esau was born, his twin brother Jacob was holding his brother's heel. This was a symbol of what was to come. In Jewish law, the elder brother inherits his father's position, but in the case of Jacob and Esau, it was Jacob who was chosen. How did this happen?

When the twins had grown, one day Esau returned from work tired and hungry. His brother Jacob had just prepared a meal, but before he would give food to his brother he demanded that Esau give him his birthright (the rights of the oldest son). Esau agreed but afterwards was sorry he had. A few years later, when Isaac was dying, Esau was again deceived by Jacob.

Isaac told Esau to prepare him a meal and that when he had done this he would give him his blessing. While Esau was gone, his mother Rebekah, who favoured Jacob, helped him to deceive Isaac into believing that Jacob was Esau. They prepared a meal and then Isaac bestowed his blessing on Jacob. When Esau returned and discovered what had happened, he was furious and vowed to kill Jacob. Jacob was forced to flee and the brothers were separated for many years. However, over time Jacob reflected on his actions and was sorry for what he had done to his brother. He apologised and eventually the brothers were reconciled. Jacob went to meet Esau and his brother rushed to him, they embraced and wept for joy.

Peace

Peace is an absence of conflict, leading to happiness and harmony. In Judaism, peace is described as one of the pillars of the world. Establishing peace on earth is one of the duties that God requires of humans. Judaism teaches that all life is sacred and respect for life requires there to be peace to enable individuals to develop morally and spiritually. A peaceful society allows people the opportunity to pursue happiness and contentment. It creates the stability for people to enjoy all aspects of life, free from violence and oppression.

Jewish teachings encourage people to make peace and be reconciled with each other. The Talmud praises the person prepared to back down in a situation of conflict. In Jewish tradition, Aaron, the brother of Moses, is regarded as the great peacemaker and provides a role model for dealing with conflicts. It was his practice to mediate between the two arguing parties and help each to understand the other's point of view, in order to bring about a peaceful reconciliation. For Jews, peace means friendship and cooperation and they believe that complete peace will only be achieved in the Messianic Age. This is a future time when God's presence will be felt by all people.

Discussion activity

Discuss the story in the case study with a partner. What does it teach about reconciliation?

Research activity

Find out about the Story of Joseph in Genesis 37–45. Write a summary of how Joseph comes to be separated from his brothers, but is eventually reconciled to them.

Activities

1. Explain why Jews believe that people should live in harmony.
2. What is meant by the term 'reconciliation'?
3. Why is reconciliation important in Judaism?
4. What is meant by peace in Judaism?
5. 'Peace is an impossible dream.' What do you think? Explain your opinion.

Beliefs and teachings

Be a follower of Aaron, love peace and pursue peace.

Rabbi Hillel

In the world to come there will be neither jealousy, hatred or rivalry.

Talmud

Speak the truth to each other and render true and sound judgement in your courts.

Zechariah 8:16

By three things is the world preserved: on justice, on truth and on peace.

Rabbi Shimon ben Gamliel

Submit to God and be at peace with him, in this way prosperity will come to you.

Job 22:21

Great peace have those who love the law, and nothing can make them stumble.

Psalm 119:165

AQA Examiner's tip

Remember when asked about peace, you need to include more explanation than just the absence of violence and war.

Summary

You should now know and understand Jewish views on reconciliation and peace.

3.3　Suffering

Suffering

Thousands homeless after earthquake strikes

Violent crime on the increase

Racist attack shocks community

School devastated by hurricane

Elderly person freezes to death in own home

Teenager attempts suicide because of bullies

A

Extension activity

Make a list of about 20 different examples of suffering.

Divide them into groups to show examples of natural causes of suffering and man-made suffering (accidental or deliberate).

Choose one example of each and describe the kind of suffering it can cause.

Could the suffering be reduced or avoided? Explain your answer.

Suffering is part of life; most people will experience some form of mental or physical pain and grief during their lives. But what is suffering? Why does it occur? Who is responsible? These are just some of the questions that need to be considered when thinking about the question of suffering in the world. For religious people, the question of suffering presents questions about the nature of God and can challenge the basis of faith. If God exists and is all-powerful and loving, then why does he allow suffering in the world? Why did God create a world in which there is so much suffering?

It is clear that suffering has many causes and that it is not always possible to prevent it from happening. Some suffering is the result of natural occurrences such as earthquakes, tsunamis, diseases and old age. These are just part of life on earth and cannot be avoided. Other suffering, however, is caused by human actions. This may be suffering caused deliberately, for example, criminal actions, war or prejudice. Sometimes people can cause suffering accidentally or without thinking about the consequences of their actions. It is simply human nature to sometimes make mistakes.

Jewish teaching

In the story of Adam and Eve (Genesis 3), Judaism teaches that suffering was brought into the world because people disobeyed God. The gift of freewill was misused and as a result human beings were separated from God. However, Jews believe that because God loves his creation, he has provided the Torah and prophets as a guide to enable people to be reconciled to him and to earn the reward of forever being in God's presence in the afterlife. The Jewish scriptures also teach that God will send a Messiah to establish his peace on earth and bring an end to all suffering.

B 'To the woman he said, 'I will greatly multiply your pain in childbearing' (Genesis 3:16)

The purpose of suffering

Throughout Jewish scriptures, there are many reasons given for the purpose of suffering: God is aware of human suffering, but people cannot hope to understand fully the divine purpose for this; suffering is a test of faith and, in the fullness of time suffering will come to an end; suffering can have many positive outcomes; it can be a test of character that brings out the good in people; suffering helps us to empathise with others and come to their aid when needed; pain and loss can make us appreciate and value what we have; a little suffering can also act as a warning to prevent something worse happening. Jews believe that suffering can help to bring them closer to God and their faith provides them with comfort and support in difficult times. Throughout Jewish history, there have been many times when Jews have encountered prejudice and persecution but their trust in God has helped to see them through.

C Tanni Grey-Thompson, paralympic gold medalist

Case study

The story of Job

The book of Job tells the story of a righteous man, who is faithful to God. It is an allegory that explains the purpose of suffering. In the story, the devil says to God that Job only worships God because his life is blessed. He had a wonderful home and family, is prosperous, respected and rich. God told the devil to do whatever he liked to Job, he would remain faithful. So the devil inflicted all kinds of suffering upon Job. In one day, he lost all his property and his children, but Job still worshipped God. So the devil filled him with disease and he suffered great pain and agony, but still he praised God. His wife and his friends questioned his faith and told him he must have sinned, but Job prayed for God to forgive them. Job never strayed from his devotion to God and was rewarded with increased prosperity and a new family.

Extension activity

Look up the story of Adam and Eve in Genesis 3. Write a summary. What do you think about the way they behaved? Do you think they deserved to be punished? Why?

Beliefs and teachings

My comfort in my suffering is this: your promise preserves my life.

Psalms 119:50

Even though I walk through the darkest valley, I will fear no evil, for you are with me.

Psalms 23:4

The Lord is righteous, yet I have rebelled against his command... look on my suffering.

Lamentations 1:18

Research activity

Find out about the story of the Exodus. In what ways does suffering feature in the story? Who suffers, who causes this and why? What do you think this story teaches about God? What can Jews learn about the purpose of suffering from this story?

AQA Examiner's tip

Using examples and quotations will help you to develop your explanation of Jewish teaching about suffering.

Activities

1 What is meant by suffering?

2 What does Judaism teach about the origin of suffering on earth?

3 What does the story of Job teach about suffering?

4 Explain, using examples, how suffering can sometimes be a positive thing.

5 'God cannot be all-loving when it is clear he lets innocent people suffer.' Do you agree? Give reasons for your answer, showing that you have thought about more than one point of view. Refer to Jewish teachings.

Summary

You should now know and understand what suffering is and Jewish attitudes to suffering.

3.4 Suffering and anti-Semitism

Anti-Semitism

Prejudice is to pre-judge someone without knowing them. It usually involves making a decision that a person or group of people is less worthy of respect simply because of, for example, their race, religion or gender. Discrimination is to treat that person or group differently because of prejudice. Throughout history, Jews have been subjected to prejudice and discrimination. The term used to describe this is **anti-Semitism**.

Throughout history, Jews have endured many attacks supported by the governments of the countries in which they lived. Some are listed below.

A History of anti-Semitism	
167 BCE	Maccabean revolt against Greek persecution
78 CE	anti-Jewish riots during the reign of Caligula
11th century	massacres and expulsions of Jews from France, Germany and Spain
12th century	massacres and expulsions of Jews from England
14th century	massacres throughout Europe, where the Jews were made scapegoats for the plague
19th century	pogroms (anti-Jewish riots) and anti-Jewish laws in Russia
20th century	the Holocaust – the Nazi policy of genocide of the Jews

Why have the Jews experienced such prejudice?

There can be no reasonable explanation for the persecution of any group of people. Anti-Semitism, like other prejudice, is a result of hatred and discrimination directed at a people simply because of their race, religious and cultural identity. Unlike other religious traditions, Jews identify themselves as a nation. They had no official homeland until the establishment of Israel in 1948. Consequently, Jews live in many countries and have a type of dual nationality, seeing themselves both as Jews and as holders of the nationality of their country. Their customs and traditions, however, mark them out as being different. At times, this has been used as an excuse for anti-Semitism, out of ignorance, upbringing or propaganda, as with the anti-Semitic material produced and broadcasted by the Nazis.

How have the Jews suffered through history?

There have been many examples of individual and national persecution of the Jewish people. During the Roman Empire, many wars were waged against the Jews, even though Roman authorities had a reputation for religious tolerance. By the Middle Ages, the Jews were dispersed around Europe and adopted the nationalities of the countries in which they lived. However, at various times they were made scapegoats for economic decline, unemployment and even plague. The resulting anti-Jewish riots led to laws restricting the freedom of Jewish people to work and practise their faith. They were subjected

A Hasidic Jews have a distinctive dress code

to massacres and forced to flee from oppression. In Russia during the 19th century, the term 'pogrom' (a pogrom is a riot directed against a particular group of people) became identified with this anti-Semitism. The press encouraged rumours that the Jews were responsible for the assassination of the Tsar, the ruler of Russia, and the poverty of the local people. A wave of anti-Jewish riots over several years devastated Jewish businesses and left thousands dead. The pogroms continued into the 20th century and many Jewish families were forced to flee to Britain and the USA to escape.

AQA *Examiner's tip*

When expressing a personal opinion on an issue, you need to include reasons for that opinion.

Case study

The diary of Anne Frank

The diary of Anne Frank tells the true story of a young Jewish girl's experience of the Holocaust. In her diary, Anne records how her family left Germany when the Nazis came to power and went to live in Holland. They settled there and were happy, but then the Nazis invaded and things began to change. Anne describes how the anti-Jewish laws that were implemented affected her life. As a Jew, she was forbidden from doing many everyday things: using buses and trams, going to the theatre, cinema and swimming pools. When the Nazis started sending the Jews in Holland to concentration camps, Anne's father made arrangements for the family to hide. For over two years, they lived in an attic apartment above where Mr Frank used to work. Despite the difficult conditions, Anne remained hopeful and wrote often of her dreams and aspirations to be a writer. However, their hiding place was discovered and Anne and her family were sent to different concentration camps. Only Mr Frank survived. When he was given his daughter's diary, which had been discovered in the attic, he published it in memory of his daughter and the millions of other men, women and children who lost their lives in the Holocaust.

Find out more at: **www.annefrank.org.uk**

Take a virtual tour at: **www.geocities.com/afdiary/places/index.html**

B   *Auschwitz concentration camp*

The Holocaust

The Holocaust is the most extreme example of anti-Semitism. After the Nazi party assumed control of Germany in 1933, a wave of anti-Jewish legislation followed. Over 400 laws were passed restricting the private and public lives of Jews. These included restricting Jewish practice in medicine, law and education and forbidding kosher laws. The Nuremburg Laws of 1935 denied them citizenship and the Nazis implemented a policy of segregation. By the time the Second World War began, the Jewish people had already suffered hugely in the ghettos they had been forced to live in. The ghettos were very crowded, and had poor living conditions. The lack of basic sanitation and appropriate healthcare facilities led to the rapid spread of disease. Over 1.5 million died in the ghettos. The Nazis' hatred of the Jews culminated in a policy known as 'the Final Solution'. The aim was to completely wipe out the Jewish people and their culture. Over 6 million Jews died, including over 1.5 million children. Today, the Jews' suffering is remembered in the UK on 27 January – Holocaust Memorial Day.

C   *Kristallnacht (the night of broken glass) 9 November 1938. Nazi attacks on the Jews*

Summary

You should now know and understand more about Jewish views and experience of suffering.

War

A war is an armed conflict between two or more countries or groups within a country. Throughout history, wars have led to immense suffering and death for millions of people. There is no single cause of a war. Wars have been fought over land, power or resources, to name but a few reasons. Many wars have been fought in the name of religion with both parties believing that God was on their side. This type of war is called a Holy War. The wars being fought today can be broadly divided into three types:

1 Wars between nations – this involves conflicts between two or more countries.

2 Civil wars – these are fought between two or more rival groups fighting for control of a country.

3 The war against terrorism – after 11 September 2001, the USA and its allies have declared war against extreme Islamic terrorists who have been responsible for horrific attacks around the world.

Modern warfare has resulted in attacks on civilians in a way that has never been seen before. Modern weapons are capable of immense destruction and loss of life. In the Second World War, the Nazis had a policy of genocide against the Jews and other groups including Romanies (who lived a gypsy lifestyle), the disabled and homosexuals. Over 6 million Jews were murdered in what is now known as the Holocaust. Genocide and ethnic cleansing are the deliberate targeting of a group of people with the aim of wiping them out. This evil aspect of modern warfare has also been seen in more recent conflicts including Bosnia, Iraq and Rwanda.

Jewish attitudes to war

Judaism teaches that war is sometimes a necessary act in order to defend justice and end oppression. The Torah makes clear that there are times when it is necessary to take up arms in order to fight for what is right. Throughout Jewish history, there are many recorded examples of the Jewish people having to fight to defend themselves and Israel (the Promised Land). For example, Joshua was commanded by God to fight to regain the land promised to their ancestors. This type of war is called an obligatory war and it is a duty for Jews to fight because it has been ordered by God.

Jewish teaching makes clear that the ideal is to have peace and that war should be avoided if at all possible. The Torah instructs rulers to offer peace before going to war. In Jewish teaching an optional war may take place only when peace has been rejected. There are also other conditions that must be met. The war must take place if the enemy starts it, because it is a religious duty to defend against aggression. It is also allowed to make a pre-emptive strike. This means that if it is known that the enemy is about to attack, defensive action can be taken to prevent this. Jews also have a duty to come to the aid of their allies if they are attacked.

A The Holocaust memorial in Miami, USA

Conduct during the war must reflect the Jewish ideals of peace and mercy. The war must be ended at the first opportunity. During the war, there must always be the possibility for those fighting to escape or surrender. It is forbidden to randomly destroy the landscape; for example, a mitzvah instructs soldiers not to uproot fruit trees. Civilians and prisoners should be treated with dignity and their basic needs provided for. It is also forbidden to fight a war to build an empire, destroy another nation, steal resources or to take revenge against an enemy. Jews believe that when the Messianic Age comes, there will be an end to all war and weapons will be turned into useful tools.

Do not destroy its trees by putting an axe to them, because you can eat their fruit.

Deuteronomy 20:19

If your enemy is hungry, give him food to eat, if he is thirsty, give him water to drink.

Proverbs 25:21

They shall beat their swords into ploughshares and their spears into pruning hooks. Nation will not take up sword against nation, nor will they train for war anymore.

Micah 4:3

Beliefs and teachings

If they refuse to make peace and they engage you in battle, lay siege to that city.

Deuteronomy 20:12

B   *Judaism teaches that peace between nations is the ideal*

War in the Old Testament

Case study

In the Old Testament there are many examples of war and at times it appears to have been a part of everyday life. There are several occasions when God commands the Israelites to go to war. In 1 Samuel 15, Saul is commanded to destroy the Amalekites because they had persecuted God's chosen people. After the conflict God is displeased with Saul because he had taken plunder from the defeated Amalekites and had not sacrificed this to Him.

David one of the most noted Kings of Israel was a great warrior. For decades the Israelites had been involved in many conflicts with the Philistines. David was a shepherd boy who came to lead the Israelites by defeating the giant Philistine, Goliath. He is described as 'A brave man and a warrior' (1 Samuel 16:18). David led many battles and in his psalms he makes clear that his victories were achieved because he had faith in God.

C   *It is forbidden to destroy fruit trees*

Activities

1   What is a war?
2   Explain three reasons why wars may take place.
3   What is genocide and ethnic cleansing?
4   Explain the Jewish teachings about war.
5   'A war should never take place unless the enemy attacks first.' Do you agree? Give reasons for your answer showing that you have thought about more than one point of view. Refer to Judaism in your answer.

Extension activity

Look up the following Psalms of David: Psalms 18, 33, 44 What do they say about Davids understanding of why he achieved military success?

Summary

You should now know and understand Jewish attitudes to war.

AQA   Examiner's tip

Remember that Judaism has obligatory and optional wars.

3.6   Nuclear war and disarmament

Nuclear war

A **nuclear war** is one in which nuclear weapons are used. The bombing of the Japanese cities of Hiroshima and Nagasaki, by the USA in the Second World War, is the only example. The horrific and devastating effects of the attack brought about an immediate surrender. These weapons are classified as Weapons of Mass Destruction (WMDs) because they are capable of killing and maiming thousands of people with a single warhead. They also have a devastating effect on the landscape and the radiation from the mushroom cloud can contaminate areas miles from the site of the attack.

Initially only a few countries had a nuclear capability, notably the USA, Russia and Britain. However, as communications and technologies have developed, a number of other countries now have nuclear capability, including Israel. Despite United Nations' treaties to reduce these weapons, there are still a growing number of nuclear weapons in more places around the world. This is known as nuclear proliferation. Many people believe that the world will never be at peace until these weapons are destroyed.

The nuclear disarmament debate

Following the devastation caused by the use of nuclear weapons in the Second World War, many people believe that they will never be used again as part of modern warfare. However, countries that do have nuclear weapons maintain that it is important to keep them, as they provide a deterrent against others developing and using them. Others argue that all countries should agree at the same time to give up these weapons. This is a process called multi-lateral **disarmament**. The United Nations has been active in developing treaties between countries to move the world towards a position where these weapons no longer exist. Most countries of the world, including Japan and the USA, have signed the nuclear non-proliferation treaty and have agreed

B A CND protest against nuclear weapons

Objectives

Understand Jewish attitudes to nuclear war and disarmament.

A A single nuclear weapon can destroy an entire city

Key terms

Nuclear war: a war in which the participants use nuclear weapons.

Disarmament: the abolition of weapons.

Research activity

1 Find out about the immediate and long-term effects of a nuclear explosion. Write a diary entry for the day that Hiroshima was attacked.

Research activity

2 Find out more about the work of the Campaign for Nuclear Disarmament (CND). Use your findings to create an information poster about the group.

not to develop these weapons. In the UK, many people, such as the Campaign for Nuclear Disarmament (CND) have argued that there should be a unilateral disarmament policy, in which the country's nuclear weapons programme is brought to an end whether or not other nations agree to do the same.

C *Arguments for and against nuclear disarmament*

Reasons against	Reasons for
Having nuclear weapons deters other countries from using them	The world leaders know they can never be used
The technology exists, it cannot be un-invented	The money spent on them could be put to better use
They have helped to keep the peace	The threat of using them is immoral
They have contributed to ending the cold war between the East and West	Peace should not be based on fear
There are other WMDs; it makes no sense to just remove one	The technology could get into the wrong hands and be used

Jewish attitudes to nuclear weapons

There are no direct references to nuclear war in Jewish sacred writings, because the issue had not arisen. However, the teachings of peace, justice and the sanctity of life make clear that the use of nuclear weapons would be very wrong. Jews believe that God has given them responsibility for the stewardship of the earth and to use weapons capable of such immense destruction would go against this. Israel, however, is believed to have a nuclear capability and is allied with the USA, which has the largest nuclear weapons programme. The issue is one of personal conscience and many Jewish people would agree with the views of those who would like to see an end to the existence of such weapons in the world. It is clear that their use could never be justified by the Jewish teachings of acceptable conduct in a war.

∞ links

See pages 76–77 for more on Jewish beliefs about stewardship.

Activities

1 What is a nuclear war?

2 Why are nuclear weapons described as weapons of mass destruction?

3 What is nuclear disarmament?

4 Explain the reasons for and against a country having nuclear weapons.

5 What is the Jewish attitude to nuclear war?

6 'Peace cannot be achieved through fear.' What do you think? Explain your opinion.

Case study

Hiroshima survivor's story

Tomiko Morimoto was just 13 years old when the atomic bomb was dropped on Hiroshima on 5 August 1945. She was in school at the time and remembers that she and her classmates were not particularly scared because the city had never been bombed, although they had heard the planes going over before. Suddenly however there was a blinding flash of light and a loud noise, then the buildings started falling down. She recalls how the teachers led them to a place of safety outside the city and that as they went there something wet like rain was coming down, but it was black. She explains how as a child she thought this was oil. They waited for their parents till the next day, but no one came.

The next day when they returned to the city, they saw the horror of the effects of the bomb. Dead people were everywhere, even people still standing up in the trams who had died the moment the bomb exploded. The river was no longer flowing, it was just a sea of dead people. Tomiko's home had been destroyed and her mother was killed. She says that surviving the bomb has made her appreciate even the smallest things in life and that she hopes the world will find peace and never again use such terrible weapons.

AQA Examiner's tip

Remember that, in some issues, believers in a faith will have differences of opinion, especially if there is no direct religious teaching on the issue.

Summary

You should now know and understand Jewish views on nuclear war and disarmament.

What is terrorism?

To be in terror is to be in complete fear. **Terrorism** is the term used to describe acts of violence carried out with the intention of intimidating and causing fear in the victims. A terrorist is anyone who plans and carries out such attacks. Most people would agree with the United Nations, who have declared that acts of terrorism are criminal activities and are a violation of human rights. Terrorism usually involves attacks that are deliberately targeted against civilians. The actions of the terrorists are intended to cause fear, injury and destruction. Attacks have included bombings, kidnapping, assassinations, hijacking and poisoning.

Terrorist groups tend to be made up of individuals with extreme and militant views. These can be related to political, ethical or religious beliefs. There are terrorist groups associated with political struggles across the world and environmental, animal rights and anti-abortion groups who use terrorist tactics to publicise their cause. There are also examples of terrorist groups like Al Qaeda, who claim to be fighting a holy war. The actions of terrorist groups are a consequence of a firm belief that what they are fighting for is right and that there is no alternative than to use violence.

The state of Israel was created in 1948 and since then has been subjected to many terrorist attacks from groups opposing Jewish ownership of the land. One of the most frequent forms of attack has been by suicide bombings. These are usually targeted at civilians and have included clubs, restaurants and buses. Suicide bombers are individuals who are prepared to die in this horrific manner for the cause they believe in. Some people argue that these activists are not terrorists but 'freedom fighters'. They see their actions as battles within a war, rather than as criminal activity.

Objectives

Understand Jewish attitudes to terrorism.

Key terms

Terrorism: when groups use violence or the threat of violence to achieve their aims, rather than using a democratic process.

A There have been hundreds of suicide bomb attacks in Israel

School children murdered as bomb explodes on morning bus

Women and children killed in Haifa Restaurant attack

Suicide bombers strike crowded Tel Aviv shopping district

C Al Qaeda caused worldwide outrage with the terrorist attack on the World Trade Centre, 11 September 2001

 B Terrorist attacks in Israel

Jewish attitudes to terrorism

The Torah teaches that peace is the will of God for all people on earth and that Jews have a responsibility to work to achieve peace. War is only justified if it is for defence or to prevent evil from occurring. The rules of war make clear that the wanton destruction of life and property is very wrong. To incite fear in innocent people and to randomly attack civilians is an act of injustice and against God. Terrorism is completely forbidden in the teachings of Judaism and the actions of terrorists should be condemned. Jews have a responsibility to fight against such evil and cowardly action and not to surrender to the evil inflicted upon them.

Beliefs and teachings

You shall not murder.

Deuteronomy 5:17

Do not accept a ransom for the life of a murderer, who deserves to die.

Numbers 35:31

Anyone tormented by the guilt of murder will seek refuge in the grave; let no one hold them back.

Proverbs 28:17

European Day for the Victims of Terrorism

Case study

On 11 March 2005, the European Community held its first day of remembrance for the victims of terrorism. This is now an annual event and the date chosen is the anniversary of the terrorist attacks in Madrid in 2004. The day is held to show support for all those who have suffered the effects of terrorist actions. It is a day to remember those who have lost their lives and to affirm the EU's commitment to democracy and human rights. It is marked with acts of commemoration throughout Europe.

What do you think? Is it a good idea to have a memorial day of this kind? What kind of activities would you suggest to mark the occasion?

Find out more about the European Network of Victims of Terrorism at:

www.giornatadellamemoria.net

Activities

1. What is terrorism?
2. Explain two reasons why some people may join a terrorist group.
3. Explain how terrorism is different to war.
4. Explain why Judaism teaches that terrorism is wrong.
5. 'Terrorists are just murderers.' Do you agree? Give reasons for your answer showing that you have thought about more than one point of view. Refer to Judaism in your answer.

∞links

For more on the Jewish teaching about war see pages 62–63.

Discussion activity

'Terrorism should not be reported in the media.'

In small groups, discuss reasons for and against this statement. Use your reasons to take part in a class debate on the issue.

D *At least 186 people were killed and more than 1000 injured in the Madrid terrorist attacks in 2004*

AQA *Examiner's tip*

Using examples will help you to explain key terms.

Summary

You should now know and understand Jewish attitudes to terrorism.

3.8 Pacifism

Pacifism

Pacifism is the belief that violence and war are wrong. Pacifists will not fight in a war and they believe that it is always wrong to kill. They also believe that there are better ways to resolve conflicts between people and nations. They believe in using non-violent action to achieve peace and resolve problems. Pacifism is not a religious belief, but a moral principle that many religious believers adopt because they believe it is in keeping with the teachings of their religion. It is connected with religious teachings such as the sanctity of life. Pacifists will not engage in war and violence because it leads to the destruction of life and encourages brutality and injustice.

Jewish attitudes to pacifism

Judaism does not teach pacifism. The Torah makes clear that there are occasions when it is a duty to fight and times where war may be a necessary evil. However, the principles of peace and justice mean that Judaism does recognise that avoiding conflict is the ideal. Throughout Jewish history, there have been many times when pacifism has been accepted as the most positive way to move forward. In the 2nd century, the Talmud records that the Jewish people took an oath of pacifism in their struggle to gain independence.

Martyrdom is when someone is prepared to die for what they believe in. It is not demanded in Judaism, with the exception of times when Jews are forced into murder, idolatry or incest. In these situations it is acceptable to take one's own life rather than commit such a grave sin. The pilgrimage site of Masada, in Israel, remembers the devotion of the Jewish people to God. Faced with the prospect of being captured and enslaved by the Romans, the occupants of Masada made the decision to sacrifice their lives rather than give in to the enemy. In such circumstances, a battle would have been pointless and would have led to suffering and death on both sides. The story explains how a small group were chosen to kill all the members of the community and then to end their own lives rather than fight the Roman legions.

Judaism teaches the right of individuals to act upon conscience. Some Jewish people may choose pacifism and there have been some famous

Objectives

Understand Jewish attitudes to pacifism.

⃝⃝ links

See Chapter 1, pages 14–15 for more on Jewish beliefs about the sanctity of life.

Key terms

Pacifism: the belief that violence and war is unnecessary and that there are other ways to resolve disputes.

A *Masada – members of the 1st-century Jewish community gave up their lives rather than fight a battle they could not win*

B *Some would rather face prison than give up their pacifist beliefs*

examples, including Albert Einstein. The Israeli government has a policy of conscription that requires all men and women over the age of 18 to serve in the Israeli military.

However, there are those who refuse to join and have served prison sentences rather than give up their pacifist beliefs. Jewish law also accepts that pacifism is a better choice than going to war, if the long-term effects of war lead to greater suffering than fighting and winning.

C Military service is compulsory in Israel

The Combatants Letter

Case study

In January 2002, over 600 Israeli soldiers signed a letter refusing to take any further part in the military operations in the occupied Gaza Strip. The document became known as the Combatants Letter and was followed by protests and demonstrations in Israel calling for an end to the hostilities in Gaza. In the letter, the soldiers reaffirm their commitment to serve to protect and defend Israel, but condemn the occupation of Gaza as against the teachings of the Jewish faith. The moving statement refers to the unjust treatment of the Palestinian people and the misery and suffering the conflict has caused to both sides. They call for the withdrawal of Israeli rule over the occupied territories and restoration of the values that should guide the Israeli Defence Forces. The actions have led to the development of the movement 'Courage to Refuse', which continues to gain support from those who believe that Israel should recognise the rights of the Palestinian people in the occupied territories.

Activities

1. What is pacifism?
2. The Israeli soldiers who wrote the Combatants Letter are not pacifists, but object to the war in Gaza. What does this example teach about Jewish attitudes to war and pacifism?
3. Explain one example of Jewish pacifism.
4. Explain Jewish teaching about pacifism.
5. 'No one should be made to serve in the armed forces.' What do you think? Explain your opinion.

Protest

What is protest?

A **protest** is any action that an individual or group may take to draw attention to an issue or cause in which they believe. Protests usually occur when people feel that an injustice has happened. Protests against injustice can be made in many different ways, from writing letters, boycotting products, joining protest groups to breaking the law and going to prison. Sometimes groups make public protests because they feel that they have no other way to make their voices heard. It is a way to attract media attention and make other people aware of the issue. Protesters think that it is right to stand up for what they believe. Sometimes people feel that it is the only way to bring about change or correct something that is wrong.

Key terms

Protest: an action to show disagreement with something, for example government policy.

A Jews protest about the conflict in Gaza

B Different forms of protest

When people are first made aware of an injustice, if they feel strongly about the matter, they will consider what action to take. They may decide to make a non-violent protest about the issue. This can be a simple action, such as signing a petition, writing to their MP or opting not to buy the goods and services of a particular company. Other forms of non-violent protest may involve more direct action: marches, sit-ins (occupying a building or space), refusing to work (for example, strike action) or causing disruption, for example, blocking roads. These actions can be very frustrating for the individuals and companies who are affected by the protests but none of them are intended to cause any direct harm to others.

Some protesters feel that non-violent actions such as these are not enough. They believe that the only way their concerns will be listened to is if they use more extreme forms of protest. This can include methods that are intended to intimidate others and force change. Change may be achieved because public opinion changes and supports the protest. On the other hand, change may be achieved as a result

Discussion activity

Discuss in small groups the various kinds of ways that protests can be made. What are the advantages and disadvantages of these forms of protest? Can violent forms of protest ever be right?

of fear, frustration or simply because the pressures caused by the protesters make it impossible to continue with a policy. Sometimes, violent protest has not succeeded because people have not been prepared to support a cause promoted through violence. However, there are many examples of protests, violent and non-violent, that have achieved their goal and brought about change.

Jewish attitudes to protest

Judaism teaches that it is right to protest against injustice and to act peacefully to bring about a resolution to wrongs. Throughout the Jewish scriptures, there are many examples of protest, including prophets questioning the acts of God. For example, in Genesis 18, Abraham pleads on behalf of Sodom and Gomorrah. In Numbers 16, Moses and Aaron fall on the ground and beg for God's mercy on sinners. In other Jewish writings, it is made clear that remaining silent, when protest is possible, is a sin.

C *Signing a petition is one way to protest*

Beliefs and teachings

Whoever can protest and does not, is accountable to his household, his community and the whole world.

Rabbinic teaching

Peace is the means for receiving God's blessings.

Misnah

Throughout history, Jews have found themselves in situations of persecution and have been subjected to unjust laws. The Jewish teachings make clear that it is right to use civil disobedience, if necessary, to protest against such injustice and to maintain the practice of faith. Civil disobedience refers to any action that is carried out against the laws of the state. In the book of Joshua, Rehab, an inhabitant of Jericho, lies to protect the Jewish spies she was harbouring, in spite of the danger this action put her in. In the Book of Esther (chapter 3), Mordechai's refusal to bow to Haman had dire consequences. In each case, the actions were prompted by the desire to do what is morally right before God. There are many such examples throughout the Jewish scriptures. However, it is also clear that such protests should be non-violent and that those protesting must do so willingly and be prepared to face the consequences of their actions.

Research activity

Find out more about the protests against the conflict in Gaza. Present your findings as a newspaper article. Including images will help to make your report more visual.

AQA Examiner's tip

Some exam questions will ask about protest in general and it will be helpful if you can give examples of different types of protest or the names of particular campaigns you have studied.

Activities

1 Explain three reasons why someone might want to protest.
2 Describe, using examples, the difference between violent and non-violent forms of protest.
3 Explain Jewish attitudes to protest.
4 'Violence should never be used to protest against injustice.' What do you think? Explain your opinion.

Extension activity

Find out more about the protests made by leading figures in the Jewish sacred writings, for example, Abraham's appeal on behalf of Sodom and Gomorrah (Genesis 18) and the protests made by some of the prophets.

Summary

You should now know about different forms of protest and understand Jewish attitudes to protest.

Reconciliation

Discussion activity

In small groups, discuss the following situations. In each case decide how the groups that are quarrelling can be reconciled to each other. Who might help them do this? How can the peace between them be kept?

- Situation one – Two school friends have an argument because one has found out that the other has been talking about him with some other friends behind his back.

- Situation two – A teacher is refusing to have a student in their class who constantly disrupts the lesson. The student wants to go back into class because she has her GCSEs coming up.

- Situation three – A group of animal rights protestors are campaigning outside the business premises of a company that deals in medical research. Their activity, if it continues, will lead to the business moving elsewhere and the loss of 300 local jobs.

- Situation four – Two countries with a history of unfriendly relations are on the brink of going to war because they each believe that the other is preparing to invade them.

Reconciliation is a process of making things right between people or groups who have disagreements. It involves humility and conscience as sometimes it can be hard to admit that an action was wrong.

Key terms

Reconciliation: when two people or groups of people who have disagreed or fought with each other make up.

Judaism teaches that there should be peace on earth and that, for people to grow morally and spiritually, there needs to be tolerance and understanding. Jews have a duty to seek to create peace on Earth because, in Jewish teaching, this is one of the pillars upon which the world stands. Human nature is such that there will inevitably be occasions when there are disagreements between people. Judaism teaches that every effort should be made to reconcile differences and create peace and harmony in society.

In the world today, Jews participate fully in world affairs. The Jewish people are spread around the world and individuals are free to pursue active roles in the governments of their nations. Israel (the only Jewish country) is actively involved in the United Nations, the world's leading organisation for world peace and security. Israel has accepted the support and guidance of other countries in attempting to bring about peaceful resolutions to the conflicts in the Middle East. Through discussion and negotiation, a number of peace treaties have been made. For example, Israel has maintained peaceful relations with Egypt and Jordan. However, there continues to be conflict in this region of the world. It is hoped that eventually reconciliation will be made to bring lasting peace and an end to hostilities.

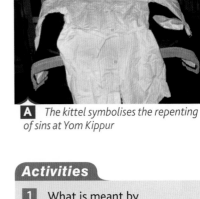

A   *The kittel symbolises the repenting of sins at Yom Kippur*

B   *The Israeli–Egyptian peace treaty ended 30 years of war*

Activities

1. What is meant by reconciliation?

2. Explain why reconciliation is important.

3. How might Jewish people show their commitment to reconciliation?

4. 'It is easier to forgive than to admit to doing wrong.' What do you think? Explain your opinion.

Yom Kippur – the day of atonement

Yom Kippur is the most sacred day in the Jewish calendar. It is a time when Jews confess their sins to God and ask for forgiveness and mercy. It is a day for prayer and reflection and when Jews make atonement for their sins. This means that they make up for what they have done wrong throughout the year. It is a form of reconciliation because it involves admitting wrongs done and committing to putting this right in the future. The day is marked by a 25-hour fast and attendance at the synagogue. Throughout the day, there are several services held in the synagogue. The doors of the ark remain open as a symbol that the gates of heaven are always open. The day concludes with the blowing of the shofar (ram's horn) and the breaking of the fast.

Find out more about the celebration of Yom Kippur. Write a diary entry for a Jewish child explaining what they have learned from the keeping of this special day.

Case study

AQA   Examiner's tip

You will not have to answer questions on Yom Kippur, but the example will help you to explain Jewish teaching about reconciliation.

Summary

You should now know about Jewish attitudes to reconciliation.

Conflict and suffering – summary

For the examination you should now be able to:

✔ know and understand Jewish views on the purpose of life, justice, reconciliation and peace

✔ understand and be able to discuss how these Jewish beliefs influence attitudes to:

– a Jewish understanding of suffering, with reference to anti-Semitism

– Jewish views about war, including disarmament, nuclear war, pacifism and terrorism

– different ways of protesting and reasons for protest

– reconciliation.

Sample answer

1 Write an answer to the following exam question:

'Explain Jewish teachings about war.'

(6 marks)

2 Read the following sample answer:

> Jews are not pacifists; they believe that it is sometimes right to go to war. In the Jewish Bible there are many examples of the Jewish people having to fight wars. Some of these wars have been ordered by God, like when Joshua attacked Jericho. Today Jews will only go to war if it is absolutely necessary. Jews believe a war is acceptable if they need to defend themselves. It is also allowed to start a war if they think that the enemy is going to attack them like when Israel invaded the Gaza strip. Jews will also fight wars together with their friends if they need their help and support to win a war against an enemy.

3 With a partner, discuss this sample answer. Do you think there are other things the student could have included in their answer?

4 What mark would you give this out of six? Look at the mark scheme in the Introduction on page 7 (AO1). What are the reasons for the mark you have given?

AQA Examination-style questions

1   Look at the photograph below and answer the following questions.

(a) Explain briefly what is meant by anti-Semitism?   *(2 marks)*

(b) Explain Jewish teaching about suffering.   *(4 marks)*

(c) 'Suffering is part of life, nothing can be done about it.' Do you agree? Give reasons
     for your answer, showing that you have thought about more than one point of view.
     Refer to Judaism in your answer.   *(6 marks)*

(d) Explain Jewish attitudes to peace and reconciliation.   *(6 marks)*

(e) 'Pacifism is the only way to achieve lasting peace. Do you agree? Give reasons for
     your answer, showing that you have thought about more than one point of view.
     Refer to Judaism in your answer.   *(6 marks)*

Examiner's tip
In section B of your exam, you will have to answer several questions requiring a longer
response. It is worth spending a few moments planning your ideas so that you can write an
organised response.

4 The environment

4.1 Stewardship

◼ What is stewardship?

The term **stewardship** means to take responsibility and care for others and their possessions. It is a key teaching within the Jewish faith and applies especially to issues related to the environment. The Jewish creation story makes clear that God created the world and gave people the responsibility of caring for the Earth. Judaism teaches that human beings are God's partners in preserving and caring for all of creation. People were given a higher status than other species and dominion over other species. This means that people have been given power by God over all other living things and have God's permission to rule and use his creation. However, stewardship and dominion should be exercised together, so this does not mean people have permission to abuse and exploit the world or the creatures in it.

Key terms

Stewardship: the belief that mankind has a responsibility to protect the world God created for them.

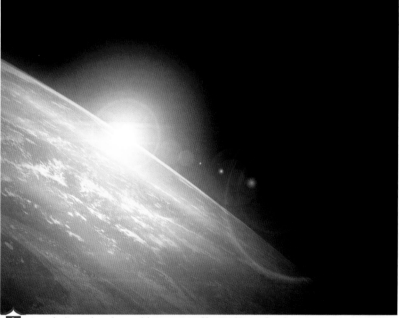

A Jews believe that the world was created by God in perfect harmony

Beliefs and teachings

Even the smallest creatures are created for the goodness of the earth. The living God did not create a single thing without a purpose.

Talmud

God said, 'Let us make man in our image, in our likeness, and let them rule over the fish of the sea and the birds of the air, over the livestock, over all the earth, and over all the creatures that move along the ground.'

Genesis 1:26

B Even the smallest creatures are created for the goodness of the Earth

Case study

The Jewish creation story and the fall

The full story can be found in the book of Genesis 1–3. There are actually two accounts of creation, but they both contain the same religious truths. The following is a summary of the teaching in the story of creation.

In the beginning there was only God who created the world from nothing. God created the heavens and the earth, the waters, the land and the sky. God filled the earth with vegetation and living creatures. The world was created in balance and harmony and God saw that it was good. God created Adam and Eve to care for creation and placed them in the Garden of Eden. They were given permission to use all of creation for their needs, but forbidden to eat from the tree of knowledge. They were given responsibility for naming all the creatures and unlike everything else, were created in the image of God. This means that they had the gift of freewill. God had given them the ability to choose between right and wrong. However, Adam and Eve sinned against God and gave in to temptation. As a punishment they were cast out of Eden, but God continues to love and care for His creation.

What does this story teach about the relationship between God and people?

Value of the natural world

Judaism teaches that the world does not belong to human beings. It is God's creation and he has entrusted people with the responsibility of stewardship of the natural world. Everything in creation has value and purpose because its existence was ordered and established by God. The natural world is essential to life on Earth and Judaism teaches that God has provided everything for the needs of human beings. The natural order of creation provides for essentials such as food, clean water and shelter. Nature also provides for emotional as well as physical needs. The beauty and serenity of the natural world is there to be enjoyed by all.

In the modern world, mankind has been able to make all kinds of advances. The technology exists to exploit the Earth's resources in a way that was unprecedented in earlier times. Where these advances benefit life on Earth, technology is a good thing; God gave to mankind the ability to reason and think. Everything created by man starts with the natural world. For example, building a car uses a wide range of natural and mineral resources. However, the exploitation of the Earth's resources has resulted in serious environmental problems, which Jews believe is a misuse of these resources. The principle of stewardship is more important than ever, if the Earth is to be preserved for future generations.

Summary

You should now know about Jewish views on stewardship and the value of the natural world.

Research activity

Look up the creation story in Genesis 1–3. Select quotes that show the main teachings that come out of this story.

C   *The natural world*

Activities

1   Explain what is meant by stewardship and dominion.
2   Explain how the teaching of the creation story encourages Jews to care for the Earth.
3   Make a list of reasons why the Earth should be valued.
4   Which do you think is the most important reason? Explain your answer.

AQA   Examiner's tip

Throughout this topic, the teaching of stewardship is important when answering questions on Jewish attitudes to the world and the environment.

■ Pollution

Pollution describes anything that contaminates the soil, water, landscape or atmosphere with harmful or unsightly results. Pollution occurs mainly because of human activity. The use of natural resources for energy, the production methods in some industries and the by-products of our lifestyles have had a massively damaging effect on our environment. This is a concern because pollution has global effects for all living things on the planet. Pollution is also responsible for some of the major environmental issues facing the world today, such as global warming, acid rain and the greenhouse effect.

Types of pollution

Pollution takes many different forms, some of which are discussed below:

Air pollution

This occurs when harmful chemicals and gases are released into the air we breathe. This is one of the most damaging types of pollution, because pollutants in the air can be carried thousands of miles. For example, in April 1986 a nuclear reactor at a power plant in Chernobyl, Ukraine exploded. The radioactive cloud from the disaster spread over many European countries affecting many people, farm animals and forests.

Water pollution

This occurs when harmful liquid waste products are released into oceans, lakes and rivers. These have an immediate and damaging effect on the water environment and spread into the soil through the water cycle. For example, algae grows rapidly as a result of the chemicals dumped in the water. This then reduces the oxygen levels in the water and kills other organisms, such as fish and coral.

Land/soil pollution

This occurs when toxic waste is buried in the ground. This causes chemical changes in the composition of the soil, making the land infertile. It also occurs with the accumulation of non-biodegradable waste. Modern manufacturing produces large quantities of materials that do not easily rot away into the soil, for example, plastics, glass and steel. These products when dumped in landfill sites, making areas of land unusable for hundreds of years.

Visual and noise pollution

These occur as a consequence of human actions. Landscapes are spoiled by the presence of open-cast mining, industrial buildings, motorways and landfill sites. The noise from industries, road networks and airports spoil the peace and tranquillity of neighbouring environments. Even in city and town environments, litter, smells from factories, smog caused by cars and industry and the noise of traffic can make for unpleasant living conditions.

Objectives

Know and understand the causes of pollution.

Know and understand Jewish attitudes to pollution.

Key terms

Pollution: harming the natural world by adding man-made toxins.

A   Car emissions are a major contributor to greenhouse gases

B   Landfill sites make areas unusable for many years

Causes of pollution

Natural disasters such as a volcanic eruption can cause pollution, but most of it is caused by human activity. Industry creates all kinds of pollution through the manufacturing process. Every day cars, buses, lorries and planes emit CO_2 gases and other fumes into the atmosphere. Lifestyles in the western world consume vast quantities of resources that produce tonnes and tonnes of rubbish. Our energy needs require the burning of fossil fuels, such as coal, that have contributed to the greenhouse effect. Millions of litres of liquid waste and sewage are poured into rivers and seas. The simple fact is that unless more effort is put into conservation and environmentally sound technologies, the earth is in danger of becoming uninhabitable!

Jewish attitudes to pollution

Judaism teaches that caring for the earth is a duty and responsibility entrusted by God. It also teaches that it is important to respect life and not to endanger living creatures. Pollution is dangerous because it affects the air we breathe, the water we drink and all aspects of the environment in which we live. Of course, Judaism would regard pollution as wrong because it is damaging to the wellbeing of life on Earth.

It is also important to consider the spiritual and moral development of people. Poor living conditions have a negative effect on people's psychological and emotional needs. A healthy environment contributes to living a healthy spiritual, as well as physical, life. A number of the Psalms make reference to the peace experienced from observing nature. For many people, nature is a way to experience awe and wonder and closeness to God.

C *Rivers and lakes are polluted with liquid waste*

Discussion activity

Discuss, in a small group, how pollution is harmful to both humans and wildlife. Share your ideas in a class discussion.

Extension activity

Working with a partner, develop a list of 'green commandments'. This should be about 10 rules that everyone should follow that would help to reduce pollution and improve the environment for everyone. Present your commandments as a colourful poster.

Beliefs and teachings

The earth is the Lord's, and everything in it.

Psalm 24:1

He makes me lie down in green pastures. He leads me beside quiet waters; he restores my soul.

Psalm 23:2–3

Activities

1 Describe the main types of pollution.
2 Explain three effects of pollution on people and the natural world.
3 Explain Jewish attitudes to pollution.
4 'Jewish people should not work for a company that is polluting the environment.' What do you think? Explain your opinion.

Research activity

Find out more about environmental issues at: www.keepbanderabeautiful.org

AQA **Examiner's tip**

When describing causes of pollution, your answers will have more depth if you can refer to different types of pollution.

Summary

You should now know about the causes of pollution and Jewish attitudes to pollution.

Consequences of pollution

Global warming

The burning of fossil fuels is contributing to the creation of a blanket of gases around the Earth, preventing harmful rays from the sun escaping out of the atmosphere. The result of this has been a gradual increase in the temperature of the planet known as the 'Greenhouse Effect'. In addition to this, the destruction of the ozone layer, which prevents harmful rays entering the Earth's atmosphere, is also adding to the problem of global warming. This is resulting in the melting of the ice caps and rising sea levels. Changes in temperatures and the effects of pollution are having devastating effects on some of the Earth's most fragile ecosystems, such as Antarctica.

When it's cold and rainy in the UK, it's easy to joke that a bit of a warmer climate would be a good thing. However, climate change is having damaging effects around the globe. Rising sea levels have resulted in increased flooding in low-lying areas and the loss of valuable farming land for vulnerable communities in poor areas, such as Bangladesh. In other areas, increased temperatures and reduced rainfall is contributing to droughts and the growth of desert areas. This leads to famine and nomadic communities being forced to give up their culture and lifestyle. There are also environmental losses as wildlife loses further habitat and eventually will be in danger of extinction.

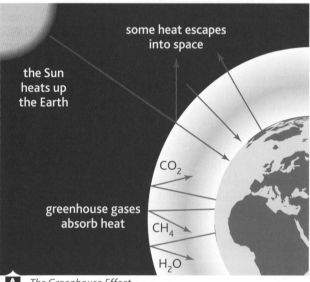

some heat escapes into space

the Sun heats up the Earth

CO_2

greenhouse gases absorb heat

CH_4

H_2O

A *The Greenhouse Effect*

Deforestation

Rainforests cover approximately 10 per cent of the Earth's land and are an essential part of regulating the Earth's climate. Trees and plant life use carbon dioxide and emit oxygen, which is essential for all animal life. This destruction of the rainforests is contributing to the effects of global warming because more carbon dioxide now remains in the air. Every year, large areas of rainforest are cleared to make way for grazing land or to provide land for industry and building. The burning of the forests also contributes to carbon dioxide pollution in the atmosphere. The rainforests lie predominantly in less developed nations, who are forced to use this natural resource in order to compete in world trade. So the pressures on people to gain enough to live on and take part in world trade leads to a reduction in the rainforests.

This is having a major impact on the environment. It is estimated that 50 per cent of the Earth's flora and fauna is found in the rainforests. The loss of habitat is leading to the extinction of species that may have been enriching the Earth in unknown ways or even, for example, holding the cure to cancer or AIDS. The increased harmful gases in the air may also be responsible for a number of illnesses caused by breathing in harmful gases, such as cancers and respiratory disorders. Native people in these areas are losing their way of life and are often

B *Rainforests cover 10 per cent of the land on Earth*

forced into a life of poverty. Wildlife is also endangered as their habitats are reduced, and there are now more species of mammals than ever in danger of extinction.

C   *Rainforests are being cleared to create grazing land*

Extension activity

Working in small groups, find out more about what sustainability means. What is being done to help protect the world's natural resources? Make a presentation to the rest of your class.

AQA   *Examiner's tip*

Refer to the effects of pollution when explaining Jewish attitudes to exploitation of the natural world.

A sustainable future

The rate at which natural resources are consumed is leading to a crisis. Fossil fuels, minerals, ores and rainforests take hundreds or even millions of years to form. Once these resources are used up, they are gone forever. We are now using these non-renewable resources at a greater rate than ever before. The excessive use is also contributing to pollution and raises questions about the impact that this will have on future generations. The need to provide for present generations needs to be balanced against the needs of people in the future. Unless action is taken now to conserve and protect natural resources, there will be long-term problems in the future.

D   *Fishing quotas help to sustain fish stocks*

Jewish attitudes

In the creation story, God commanded people to fill the world and take control of it and he made them stewards over all that was made. God also gave human beings the reason and intelligence to do this wisely. The Jewish teaching of tzedaka, meaning justice, should be applied to all human actions including those that have an impact on the environment. Jews believe that they have a responsibility to act with justice in the world. The effects of pollution undermine the principles of justice and fair treatment of all living things. Global warming and deforestation are affecting many vulnerable people and destroying habitats, which is wrong. Judaism teaches that the environment can be used to meet people's needs but that it should not be exploited for human greed and desires. The responsibility of stewardship also extends to preserving the world for future generations to come.

Activities

1   How does pollution contribute to global warming?

2   Explain **three** effects of the destruction of the rainforests.

3   What is sustainability and why would Jews believe this is an important idea?

4   Explain why Judaism teaches that harming the environment is wrong.

5   'The needs of people are more important than the environment.' What do you think? Explain your opinion.

Summary

You should now know about Jewish attitudes to pollution and its effects.

4.4 Conservation

The conservation movement

Conservation has become one of the most pressing concerns facing the modern world. The devastating effects of pollution and the exploitation of the natural world means that action must be taken to preserve the Earth's dwindling natural resources. Conservation policies are a concern for all the countries of the world. Action is needed now to ensure that a balance between the needs of the present and those of future generations can be met.

The **environmental conservation** movement seeks to address the many environmental issues. It is concerned with protecting natural fragile environments such as the rainforests and Antarctica. It is also involved with projects to preserve and protect animals and other species in danger of extinction because of the effects of hunting and habitat loss. Conservation also involves finding ways to manage industries that rely on non-renewable resources, such as fossil fuels, and those which are in danger of over-exploiting stocks, such as fishing and timber. It will take a long time to repair the damage already inflicted on the natural world, but with international cooperation the aims of the conservation movement can be met.

Jewish attitudes to conservation

The teaching of stewardship means that conservation and developing a sustainable future are important in Judaism. The Earth was created by God and Jews believe that they are partners with God in preserving the natural world. Many Jewish teachings illustrate the importance of caring for animals and the environment. An act of Tikkun Olam, which means 'repairing the world', draws people closer to God. This means that by making the effort to do things that help to preserve the environment, a person can develop their relationship with God.

Objectives

Understand Jewish attitudes to conservation.

Key terms

Conservation: protecting the natural world.

Environmental conservation: looking after the natural resources of the planet by taking steps to conserve them.

⭕links

For more on stewardship see pages 76–77.

A   *Replanting fallen trees is one type of conservation project*

B   *Alternative sources of energy such as solar panels, relieves the pressure on non-renewable resources*

Participating in conservation projects or simply striving to be eco-friendly at home are ways that people can demonstrate their commitment to stewardship and devotion to God. The importance of conservation is also seen in the mitzvoth to make a migrash – an area of open land between towns. This is an instruction in the Jewish teachings that requires there to be grazing land between towns, rather like the 'green belt' that protects rural areas in the UK.

When it comes to conservation, the law of bal tashchit, meaning 'do not destroy', is also important. The Jewish scriptures forbid the deliberate destruction of trees and this principle can be applied to other aspects of creation. Judaism teaches that it is wrong to wantonly destroy nature and that it is important to conserve resources to meet human needs. The many teachings relating to the care of animals also indicate that it is important to protect endangered species. In the story of the flood, Noah was told to save every species of animal and the rainbow is a symbol of the covenant between God and man that included the promise to never again destroy the earth.

C *The rainbow is a reminder of the covenant between God and Noah*

Beliefs and teachings

The sign of the covenant (a rainbow) I make between me, you, all living things and future generations never to again destroy the earth.

Genesis 9:11–12

Research activity

Research the work of the World Wildlife Fund (WWF). Make a presentation about some of the species of animals in danger of extinction and what is being done to stop this happening.

Activities

1. What is meant by the term 'conservation'?
2. Why is conservation important?
3. Explain Jewish teachings about conservation.
4. 'Conservation should come before human needs.' Do you agree? Give reasons for your answer, showing that you have thought about more than one point of view. Refer to Judaism in your answer.

Extension activity

Imagine that you have been invited to give a talk to Jewish primary school children about the importance of conservation. Prepare the presentation you would give. Remember to include some references to Jewish teachings and make sure that you explain these ideas very simply, so the children will be able to understand.

AQA Examiner's tip

When evaluating, you need to make sure that you consider at least two different viewpoints, even if you do not agree with one of them.

Summary

You should now know about conservation and Jewish attitudes to this issue.

Participation in conservation

Individual responses

As stewards of the Earth, Judaism teaches that all Jews have a responsibility to do what they can to help conserve the planet. In the home, many Jewish families will do their part by trying to avoid needless waste and recycling what they can. The Torah makes clear that needless destruction is wrong and, by acting in an eco-friendly way, Jews can play their part in preserving resources for the future. Today, there is lots of information and advice for everyone on how they can reduce their carbon footprint.

Recycle things like glass, paper, cans	Buy products with less packaging
Choose products that are recycled or from sustainable sources	Avoid waste by using what is needed and limiting excess
Cut fuel consumption in the home and travelling	Reuse carrier bags, make compost
Give to charity shops rather than throw away	Support environmental initiatives locally and globally

  A   *Tips for reducing your carbon footprint*

B   *Recycling is one way of participating in conservation*

Community responses

Throughout the Torah, there are many teachings that demonstrate that the Jewish community must take a collective responsibility for creation. During wartime, there is a commandment not to destroy the fruit trees to build battlements. In Numbers 35, the principle of migrash requires that open land is left between cities, rather like the principle of having a greenbelt today. The Talmud further instructs the planting of trees around cities to enhance the environment. Many of the Psalms make reference to the wonder of creation and its importance for the spiritual needs of mankind.

Judaism recognises that to deal with major environmental issues, there needs to be a collaborative approach between all the nations of the world. In 1986, leaders from the Jewish community joined with members of all faiths at a special conference held by the WWF in Assisi. Its aim was to produce a faith response to environmental issues. This has become known as The Assisi Declarations and includes teachings from all of the world's major faith traditions.

Objectives

Know and understand Jewish responses to conservation.

Discussion activity

In a small group, discuss the suggestions for being eco-friendly. What are their advantages and disadvantages? Can you think of any other ways to be eco-friendly? Share your ideas with the rest of the class.

Jewish statement from Assisi

In the Assisi declarations, the teachings of Judaism set out the Jewish attitude to the environment. The world is the creation of God, who has provided it for the use of mankind. In the future, God will judge all people on their actions and intentions. The Earth is provided for our needs and God has made people responsible as leaders and custodians of his creation. To be obedient to God's commands is a joyful experience and is the way to become closer to God. The environmental problems facing the world today should be a concern for all Jewish people. God expects people to be righteous and to use the dominion he gifted to mankind with justice and compassion. Human beings will be acting responsibly only if they act in good conscience.

C   *Many Jewish prophets were shepherds*

Beliefs and teachings

The whole land will be laid waste because there is no one who cares.

Jeremiah 12:11

To serve G-d, one needs access to the beauties of nature... these are essential to the spiritual development of people.

Rabbi Abraham ben Moses

Research activity 🔍

Research the work of the Coalition of the Environment and Jewish Life (COEJL). Look at their website at www.coejl.org

Write a summary of the work they do to support conservation initiatives.

Activities

1. Explain three ways that Jewish families can contribute to conservation efforts.
2. Explain the Jewish teaching on the environment made at Assisi.
3. Copy out the two quotations on this page. How could they be applied to the issue of conservation?
4. 'Conservation is good for the soul as well as the planet.' How far do you agree? Give reasons for your answer, showing that you have thought about more than one point of view. Refer to Judaism in your answer.

D   *Composting food waste helps to reduce your carbon footprint*

AQA Examiner's tip

You can include spiritual reasons for conservation as well as practical ones in your answers.

Summary

You should now know about Jewish responses to conservation.

Reflections on the environment

Festivals in Judaism

Festivals play an important part in the Jewish calendar and are a time for families and the community to come together to remember important events in Jewish history with worship and celebration. They are particularly enjoyed by children. Festivals also give Jews an opportunity to reflect upon their relationship with God and, in the case of certain festivals, their relationship with the natural world. We will look in particular at the festivals of Sukkoth and Tu B'Shevat.

Objectives

Understand Jewish attitudes to the environment through a study of the celebration of the festivals of Sukkoth and Tu B'Shevat.

Sukkoth

Sukkoth, or Tabernacle, is the Jewish harvest festival. It is celebrated in the Jewish month of Tishrei around September/October. It is a time when Jews remember their ancestors living in the wilderness after escaping from Egypt. Throughout the week of the celebration of the festival, Jews are reminded that God cares and provides for them. The building of the Sukkah, an outdoor shelter, and the time spent there is a way of engaging with nature and remembering the beauty of the natural world.

> I love this festival because it's fun spending time in the Sukkah, it's like it's a den. It's good to be outside looking at the stars and enjoying the fresh air. It feels more special with everyone together eating and enjoying themselves. It makes a change to be away from the TV and computer games and to enjoy the outdoors.

A Sukkah – a child's view

Sukkoth celebrations

A Sukkah is a temporary shelter covered with leaves. At the start of Sukkoth, Jewish families build such shelters in their gardens and shelters will also be erected at the synagogue. The most important feature is a roof made of a thin covering of leaves so that the sky can still be seen. This will be decorated with fruit hanging from the leaves. During the week, all meals, worship and entertaining will take place there.

Every day except Shabbat, a special harvest service is conducted. The symbols of the 'four species' – a lemon, a palm leaf, sprigs of willow and myrtle are held by the leader of the service, usually the father in the home. As prayers for rain are said, he will move these in many directions to symbolise that God's presence can be felt everywhere. The people are reminded of his blessings and the goodness of all creation. Sukkoth is a time to reflect on the wonder, beauty and importance of creation. It is a time to remember that God has provided all that people need. In modern times, it is also a time to think about the importance of conserving the world and helping to contribute to reducing some of the environmental problems that exist today.

B A Jewish father in a Sukkah holding the 'four species'

Tu B'Shevat

On the 15th day of the Jewish month of Shevat (January–February), the festival of Tu B'Shevat is celebrated. This is known as New Year for Trees. Its original purpose was to calculate the age of trees to fulfil the commandment in Leviticus. Traditionally, it is customary to eat dried fruit and nuts on this day and some people plant trees. Jewish children may go round collecting money to have trees planted in Israel.

This is a minor festival in the Jewish calendar and so it may be that the synagogue service nearest to the date will be used to reflect on the importance of the environment. The sermon may include references to the teachings of the Torah related to the care of the environment. The Rabbi may choose to use this opportunity to remind the congregation of their responsibilities as stewards of God's creation.

C   *Allowing fruit trees to establish themselves leads to better harvests*

Beliefs and teachings

When you enter the land and plant any kind of fruit tree, regard its fruit as forbidden. For three years you are to consider it forbidden; it must not be eaten. In the fourth year all its fruit will be holy, an offering of praise to the LORD. But in the fifth year you may eat its fruit. In this way your harvest will be increased. I am the LORD your God.

Leviticus 19:23–25

Discussion activity

How do these two festivals help Jewish children to understand the importance of the natural world?

Activities

1   How do the celebrations of Sukkoth and Tu B'Shevat remind Jews of their relationship with:
   - God
   - the environment?

2   Write a diary for a Jewish child, reflecting on their week living in the sukkah.

3   'Celebrating festivals isn't going to do anything to stop environmental destruction.' What do you think? Explain your answer, showing that you have thought about more than one point of view. Refer to Judaism in your answer.

Extension activity

Design a suitable Sukkah that could be put up at your home. Draw and label the design and write an explanation of the times you would use it and the possible problems you may have to anticipate.

AQA   Examiner's tip

You will not be specifically examined on the knowledge of these two festivals but your study will help understanding Jewish attitudes to the environment.

Summary

You should now understand how Jewish festivals contribute to Jewish attitudes to the environment.

Animal rights

It is clear that people share some of the same attributes as animals, such as the basic characteristics of all living things. Like human beings, animals breathe, move, grow; they need to eat, excrete and reproduce. They are also sentient beings with the ability to feel pleasure and pain. Animals are able to communicate and live in social groups, demonstrating some of the characteristics associated with human families. They are also able to express emotions and feelings, even though their reactions are innate rather than the product of reasoned thought. Given that animals have so much in common with human beings, should they also have **rights**?

The use of animals

We share the planet with thousands of different species of living things. Mammals, sea creatures, birds, even the tiniest insects; all have a part to play in the ecology of the natural world. Every living thing is part of an eco-system and contributes to making the environment work. People use animals in many ways, for work, companionship, food and clothing to name but a few. Some of these uses are to meet human needs and many people would not consider them to be wrong. However, other uses can seem very cruel and appear to be for no other reason than to provide pleasure for people at the expense of animal suffering. Many people consider human life to be more important than animal life, but does that give us the right to use animals in any way we choose?

What are animal rights?

The term 'rights' is linked to ideas of justice and fairness. It means to have legal or moral protection. Whether or not animals should have rights is an ethical question; it involves deciding if there can be right or wrong ways to treat animals. There are a wide range of views on

A *Animals are able to express feelings and emotions*

B *Is it right to make animals perform for human entertainment?*

this issue. Some people are animal liberationists and feel that animals should be treated equally with human beings and are prepared to go to extreme lengths to campaign for what they believe in. For example, they believe it is right to protest against what they see as misuse of animals by attacking organisations and individuals who use animals for research or participate in hunting. At the other end of the scale, there are people who feel that animals are there to be used in any way humans choose.

Discussion activity

2   How far do you agree with the views of these four people? What is your view of the use on animals?

> I am an animal rights activist. Animals cannot speak for themselves so they need people like me to stand up for them. I see nothing wrong with disrupting businesses which make money out of the suffering of innocent animals. I am prepared to go to prison if I have to. Someone has to make a stand against animal abuse.

> I am a vegetarian. I do not eat animals because it is wrong to kill; all life is valuable. I believe animals should be treated with respect. I would like to see a world where people work with animals sharing the planet and not causing unnecessary suffering. There is nothing wrong with having pets and using animals for work, but they must be properly cared for.

> I think animals should have some rights. In this day and age, animals shouldn't be being abused just for entertainment. Wild animals need protection; otherwise some species are going to become extinct. I don't think it's wrong to use animals for human needs such as for food, as we are the superior species, but I don't think there should be unnecessary cruelty.

> Animals are there for us to use. They aren't the same as people and I don't think it matters how we use them. They are a resource just like everything else on the planet. I think there are more important issues to address than animal rights. What's the point in making laws to ban hunting when there are thousands of homeless people on the streets?

 C   *Views on animal rights*

Jewish attitudes

Judaism teaches that animals are an important part of creation and that people have a responsibility to care for animals and treat them with respect. Jews believe in the sanctity of life and that human life is more valuable than that of animals. However, this does not mean that animals can be treated inhumanely and exploited for human greed and desires. There are many teachings within Judaism about the care of animals and the need for compassion to be shown. These teachings could be regarded as rights that all animals should be given when being used by humans.

Research activity

Choose five of the ways that people use animals and find out about Jewish attitudes to them. Make a leaflet to explain the Jewish views and try to include some teachings from the Jewish sacred writings.

Activities

1   How do humans use animals?
2   Why do some people think animals should have rights?
3   What does Judaism teach about animal rights?
4   'People are more important than animals.' What do you think? Explain your opinion.

Beliefs and teachings

Six days you shall do work, but on the seventh day you rest so that your ox and your donkey may rest.

Exodus 23:12

Do not plow with an ox and a donkey yoked together.

Deuteronomy 22:10

Do not slaughter a cow or a sheep and its young on the same day.

Leviticus 22:28

Do not muzzle an ox while it is treading out the grain.

Deuteronomy 25:4

AQA *Examiner's tip*

When discussing controversial issues, make sure that you give reasons and produce evidence and do not just state your personal opinion.

Summary

You should now understand the term 'animal rights' and know that there are different views on the rights of animals.

Jewish teaching

Objectives

Understand Jewish attitudes to the care of animals.

Within Judaism, there are many teachings relating to animals. The creation story makes it clear that people have power and responsibility over animals and are more greatly valued by God. However, it is also clear that the responsibility of stewardship means that it is wrong to misuse animals and treat them badly. The teaching of Tza'ar Ba'alei Chayim literally means 'the suffering of living creatures' and underpins Jewish teaching about the proper care of animals. Judaism recognises that animals are living, feeling beings created by God. It is strictly forbidden in Judaism to deliberately cause harm to animals.

The Torah makes clear that human beings have responsibilities when caring for their animals. The commandment to rest on the Sabbath day should also be applied to animals. After labouring in the fields, a man must make provision for his animals before himself. The feelings of animals are also recognised in the mitzvoth. For example, laws forbid using male and female animals together and the killing of young animals in front of the mother. Jews are reminded to care for animals in need, even if they belong to their enemies.

A Working animals must be treated with respect

The teachings of Judaism means that many of the ways in which animals are exploited today are considered wrong. Destroying habitats leading to the extinction of species is offensive to God. Using animals for blood sports or as cheap entertainment in circuses goes against the principles of stewardship and Tza'ar Ba'alei Chayim. Jews are allowed to keep pets and domesticated animals, but they must be properly cared for. Keeping animals in zoos and nature reserves is acceptable if their aim is to conserve and protect the animals.

Beliefs and teachings

Give grass in your fields for your cattle, and then you shall eat and be full.

Deuteronomy 11:15

A righteous man cares for the needs of his animal.

Proverbs 12:10

Extension activity

1 Working with a partner, make up a list of about 10 rules for the proper treatment of animals. These rules should reflect Jewish teaching about caring for animals.

B Pets must be properly cared for

Jewish attitudes to eating meat

At the time of creation, human beings were only given permission to eat vegetation food; only after the flood did God give permission to eat meat. This was accompanied by strict rules regarding the slaughter of animals, the purpose of which is to reduce the animals' suffering. Some Jews choose to live as vegetarians but this is a matter of personal conscience. Many are meat eaters and adhere to the Jewish food laws. This means that the farming methods used must be in keeping with the kosher food laws. The methods of intensive farming conflict with the fair and compassionate treatment of animals.

C   *Organic free-range products respect animal welfare*

Research activity

Research Jewish food laws including the meaning of Kosher, Kashrut and Treyfah. Present your findings as a leaflet with a suggested menu for the day.

Beliefs and teachings

Every thing that lives will be food for you. Just as I gave you the green plants I now give you everything.

Genesis 9:3

Do not cook a young goat in its mother's milk.

Exodus 34:26

Activities

1 Explain Jewish teaching about the care of animals.
2 Why do you think some Jewish people choose to be vegetarians?
3 'You cannot eat meat and call yourself an animal lover.' What do you think? Explain your opinion.

Extension activity

2 Working in small groups, research some suitable recipes that would meet the requirements of Jewish food laws. Use your findings to make a Jewish recipe book.

   Cross-curriculum links – if you are studying Food Technology, you could try making one of the recipes and bring it into class for everyone to try.

D   *Battery hens – an example of intensive farming*

AQA Examiner's tip

Referring to Jewish teaching in your answers helps to demonstrate understanding.

Summary

You should now know about Jewish attitudes to the care of animals.

Using animals for research

Using animals for research

Every year, millions of animals are used to conduct experiments to further human knowledge and understanding of the world in which we live. Most animals used in research are bred specifically for that purpose and the experiments involving higher-order mammals are a very small percentage of the total animals used. In some countries, there are strict regulations about the use of animals in research but some people feel that this is not enough and that all animal experimentation should be stopped.

I think that it is right to experiment on animals because it is important to save human lives. Medicine would not advance if these experiments were not conducted. They are essential for developing new drugs and medical procedures such as transplant surgery. The animals used are bred for that purpose and are mostly just rats and mice. Mammals are only used when they have to be and there are laws to make sure the animals' suffering is kept to a minimum. At the end of the day human life is more important. A few animals dying is worth it if it helps us cure cancer.

I think it is always wrong to experiment on animals, it is cruel and inhumane. Lots of research is conducted for pointless things like cosmetics and the effects of smoking. There is lots of new technology these days, so there is no need to use animals. In any case, animals' physiology is different from ours, they don't respond the same. If they had tested penicillin on guinea pigs, we might never have had it as a medicine because it is fatal to them. All animals are important and should be treated with respect; cruelty to animals is no different to cruelty to children.

A Reasons for and against using animals in research

Jewish attitudes

Judaism does not consider animals to be equal to humans and so does not forbid the use of animals for research providing the reason is a good one. If research using animals is necessary to alleviate human suffering, such as in the advance of medicine, then it is permitted. Where experimenting on animals is necessary, Judaism teaches that animal suffering must be kept to a minimum. Tests should not be pointlessly repeated, unnecessarily cruel or conducted when the benefit to humans is unclear.

B Cosmetics are sometimes tested on animals

The Torah makes clear that compassion should be shown and so it would be wrong to experiment on animals where there are alternatives to this. Experimenting on animals to satisfy human curiosity or for unnecessary human vanity such as make-up and perfumes is also wrong. Many Jews consider it wrong for students to conduct experiments on animals when this could be done using computers. Similarly, many Jews would support campaigns to end cosmetic testing and advocate buying products that have not been produced causing suffering to animals.

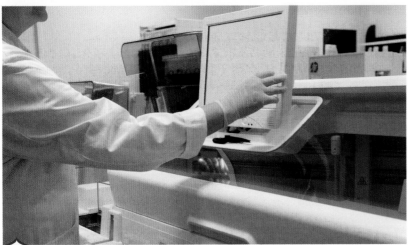

C   *New technology is reducing the need for animal experimentation*

Discussion activity

'This house believes that all experiments on animals should be banned.'
Prepare arguments for and against this statement. Hold a class debate
and take a vote at the end. Vote on the quality of the arguments made,
rather than what you may personally believe is correct.

Beliefs and teachings

It is forbidden to cause pain to any animal.

Maimonedes Code

God's teaching requires you to refrain from inflicting unnecessary pain on
any animal and to help lesson pain where you see animals suffering.

Rabbi Hirsch

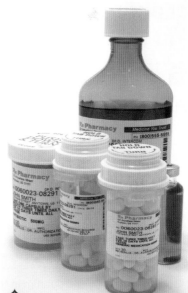

D   *Is animal testing necessary for medicine to advance?*

Activities

1   What does using animals for research involve?
2   Why is it an ethical concern?
3   Explain Jewish teaching about experimenting on animals.
4   'If human lives are saved, then it is not wrong to experiment on
    animals.' Do you agree? Give reasons for your answer, showing
    that you have thought about more than one point of view. Refer to
    Judaism in your answer.

Extension activity

Imagine that you have just read in your local newspaper about a protest
held in support of banning experiments on animals. Write a letter for the
newspapers 'Readers' letters' page, saying why you agreed or disagreed
with the protest that was held.

AQA Examiner's tip

When discussing the use of
animals for research, remember
that Jewish attitudes vary
depending on whether the
research is for medical or cosmetic
purposes.

Summary

You should now know and understand Jewish attitudes to the use of
animals for research.

4.10 Stewardship conclusions

Stewardship

New research shows sea levels are rising

Greenbelt land needed for new homes

Tests on animals confirm safety of new cancer drug

Hunting ban has lead to job losses

A

B *All creation belongs to God*

When the scriptures were written, the environmental issues facing the world today did not exist. However, throughout the scriptures, there are many references to the natural world that Jews can use to guide them in their understanding and attitudes to the environment. Jewish teachings and history address the relationship that exists between God, people and the natural world. It is clear that the ideal of creation is a world in balance and harmony, that creation belongs to God and that people are partners with God in the care and protection of all living things. The role of stewardship is therefore a sacred duty.

Beliefs and teachings

God took the man and put him in the Garden of Eden to work it and take care of it.

Genesis 2:7

God formed the man from the dust of the ground and breathed into his nostrils the breath of life.

Genesis 2:15

Give them pasturelands around the towns.

Numbers 35:2

Jews believe that human beings are unique in creation and have been chosen by God to be set apart from all other species. God created man in his own image and breathed life into him. He offered to his people the gift of freewill, giving people the opportunity to reason and make choices of their own. The unique power of human beings is to be able to rule and dominate the rest of creation for their benefit. However, the value of creation is also recognised and God created everything for a purpose. In using creation, people must also be aware of their responsibilities as stewards.

It is sometimes difficult to balance the needs of human beings against those of the rest of creation. Human life is sacred and Judaism teaches

C *Stewardship involves working in harmony with nature*

that human life has priority over all other living things. However, dominion or rule over the rest of creation does not entitle people to abuse and exploit the natural world. The final day of creation was a day of rest; no work is to be done on this day. Similarly, the Torah instructs farmers to let the fields rest every seventh year. Transport systems and industry are major contributors to pollution. If the world observed a day of rest each week, creation too might be given a chance to recover.

Jews believe that God has given permission for people to use and enjoy his creation, but they are only tenants on the earth, not owners. It is wrong to waste, exploit or needlessly destroy anything in creation. The Koheleth Rabbah (a Jewish writing explaining Ecclesiastes), explains that when God first created Adam and Eve, he walked them round the garden of Eden and made them aware of the beauty and good of creation and warned them not to destroy it because it would not be repaired. The present environmental crisis is a consequence of wrongful human action. It is therefore the responsibility of people to put things right for God, for others and for future generations.

People are more important than animals.

Global warming is a punishment from God.

The extinction of species is an insult to God.

Sacred writings cannot help to solve environmental issues.

D   *How far would Judaism agree?*

E   *God saw that his creation was good*

Activities

1. For each of the statements on the tree in Illustration D, explain how far Jewish attitudes would agree with the statement.

2. Now repeat the task for your views of the statements.

3. Use the information on this page to write a leaflet explaining Jewish attitudes to the environment.

4. 'A day of rest would do more for creation than any conservation project.' How far do you agree? Give reasons for your answer, showing that you have thought about more than one point of view. Refer to Judaism in your answer.

Extension activity

For religious believers, prayer is an important way to reflect. Write a prayer for the environment that could be used by Jewish children.

Summary

You should now know and understand about Jewish attitudes to stewardship.

AQA   Examiner's tip

Evaluations need to include reference to Jewish beliefs and attitudes to the issue.

4

Chapter 4: The environment – summary

For the examination you should now be able to:

✔ show understanding of how Jewish views on stewardship and the value of the natural world influence Jewish attitudes to:

– the created world
– reasons why the created world is valued by Jews
– causes of pollution
– conservation
– animal rights
– care of animals
– using animals in research
– stewardship.

Sample answer

1 Write an answer to the following exam question:

Explain Jewish teaching about stewardship. Use examples of stewardship in your answer.

(*6 marks*)

2 Read the following sample answer:

In the Jewish creation story Adam and Eve are made God's stewards of the Earth. The story tells how God has created the world in 6 days and made a day of rest on the 7th. The world was created beautifully and was perfect and God gave it to them to use and look after. But Adam and Eve disobeyed God and they got sent out of Eden. Some Jewish people think this is why there are so many problems in the world, because people disobey God. If you think about it, this is right

because God said to look after the trees but we are chopping down the rainforests. Stewardship is all about looking after the world because it belongs to God and Jews think it is very important to do this. That's why they have a festival where they plant trees and they have rules saying you can't just cut them down when you feel like it. I think it's a really good idea and it is one way that people can be good stewards to the earth.

3 With a partner, discuss the sample answer. Do you think there are other things that the student could have included in their answer?

4 What mark would you give this answer out of six? Look at the mark scheme in the introduction on page 7 (AO1). What are the reasons for the mark that you have given?

AQA Examination-style questions

1   Look at the photograph below and answer the following questions.

(a)   Explain Jewish attitudes to animal rights.   *(3 marks)*

(b)   'Jewish people should be vegetarians.' What do you think? Explain your opinion.   *(3 marks)*

(c)   Explain how pollution is damaging the environment.   *(3 marks)*

(d)   Explain Jewish responses to conservation.   *(4 marks)*

Examiner's tip   In section A, questions will be structured in different ways to include short and long answers. You need to learn what the command words, such as explain or describe, require you to do.

5 Crime and punishment

5.1 Jewish views on the law

■ The Jewish law

As you already know, Jews have 613 mitzvoth (laws), given to them by God via Moses and recorded in the Torah. Of these 613 mitzvoth, 365 are negative, telling Jews what they must not do, while 248 are positive. Some of them refer to religious observance such as Shabbat and sacrifices (which Jews have not offered since the destruction of the Temple in 70 CE), rather than to day-to-day living.

The mitzvoth are aimed at improving the quality of society by creating a world as God wants it to be. They are also intended to save life. The only three that cannot be broken in order to save life are:

- You shall not murder.
- You shall not make for yourself any idol.
- You shall not commit adultery.

However, laws cannot exist without punishments. If a person breaks the law, whether it is a religious law or a criminal one, unless punishment follows, there is less incentive to actually obey the law. The potential punishments that God could impose for serious breaches of his law are much greater than punishments that people can impose for breaches of criminal law. However, the mitzvoth impose severe punishments, many of which are deemed to be inappropriate in modern society.

■ The state law

There are Jews living in many different countries, all with different sets of laws. Some of these countries have some laws that are against Jewish law. In Britain, there are no restrictions about what can be done on a Saturday (Shabbat) and meat sold in butchers and supermarkets is usually not slaughtered in accordance with Kashrut rules as set out in the Torah. However, this does not stop Jews following their religious law if they choose to. They can keep Shabbat as a day of rest and religious observance and use a kosher butcher for their meat. This is not illegal, so there is no conflict between the mitzvoth and British law in these instances.

There are some instances where Jewish law does appear to come into conflict with British law but these often refer to situations that no longer apply to the Jewish way of life. For example, the Torah lays down several rules about the treatment of slaves, which were designed to improve the life of a slave. However, keeping slaves is illegal in Britain so these rules refer to a practice that is illegal. This does not matter to Jews though because they no longer keep slaves anyway and none of the rules say that they should!

A The mitzvoth are found in the Torah

Even though they are open on Saturday, it doesn't mean we have to shop there on a Saturday

B

Despite differences between Jewish law and state law, Jews are taught to accept the law of the land but to protest about any areas of it that are against Jewish principles, prevent them from practising their faith or promote injustice.

Activities

1   Explain the purpose of the mitzvoth.
2   Do you think that the instruction to obey the law of the land and protest if it is against Jewish principles is a good one? Explain your reasons.
3   Are there any laws that go against your principles? If so, what are they and why are they against your principles? If not, explain why not.

The Bet Din

The Bet Din is a Jewish court presided over by rabbis that give rulings on religious or civil matters. This includes certifying foods to be kosher, treif (non-kosher) or parve (neutral as not containing either milk or meat). They also resolve civil disputes over matters such as business or divorce involving Jewish people. In Britain, they are allowed to make such rulings but cannot make judgements on criminal matters. Jewish people may have their own reasons for using the Bet Din, but foremost in many people's minds is the belief that the Bet Din is doing God's work and uses interpretations of religious experts rather than a civil court that has no understanding of Judaism. In order for their judgements to be binding, both sides must be Jewish and in agreement with the matter being heard by the Bet Din.

∞ links

See pages 122–123 for more on Jewish beliefs about divorce.

Activity

4   Do you agree that Jews should be allowed to use the Bet Din to rule on religious or civil matters? Explain your reasons.

Ruth and Jacob

Jewish couple Ruth and Jacob married in 1996 but over the 12 years they were married, seemed to drift apart. Jacob's work kept him away from home more than either of them wished but he didn't feel that he could change the job that he otherwise enjoyed and which provided a comfortable lifestyle for them both. Sons Adam and Daniel found it increasingly difficult growing up in a home where their mother and father argued and clearly had 'fallen out of love'. After a great deal of discussion over several weeks in 2005, they decided to separate with a view to getting divorced at a later date.

In 2007, they decided to divorce. They applied to the Bet Din because they wanted to follow the procedures laid down in their faith properly. In February 2008, the Bet Din granted them a divorce which they both accepted. They knew though that this was not legally binding in Britain so obtained a civil divorce to show they were divorced legally in the eyes of the state in addition to religiously in the eyes of God through the Bet Din.

C   *Ruth and Jacob were granted a divorce by the Bet Din*

Case study

Summary

You should now have more knowledge and understanding of Jewish law and its relationship with state law.

What causes crime?

A   *Why is this crime being committed?*

Many scholars have analysed the causes of crime. Their reasoning is that if they can find out what causes crime, there is a chance that potential offenders' needs can be addressed, and they can be persuaded not to commit crime again. While this could never be completely effective, any reduction in crime is welcomed by society and by the individuals most affected by it. Some of the causes of crime have been identified as:

- **Poverty** – some commit crime because they do not have sufficient money to cover their needs or, in some cases, to provide extra things that they want. They may have grown up in a poor family or their parents may have been involved in dishonest activities and they are following their parents' example.

- **Addiction** – possession and dealing in illegal drugs are offences that carry serious punishments. In addition, people who are addicted to drugs have no choice but to obtain them. If they cannot afford to buy them, the temptation to turn to crime to obtain money is very strong. This also includes offences committed while under the effects of alcohol – a contributory factor to many crimes.

B   *Some offenders commit crime to give them a 'buzz'*

- **Peer pressure** – many young people who become involved in gangs do so because they have friends in gangs and join because they do not want to be seen as weak. Some others join a gang because they feel it offers them safety. While gangs themselves are not illegal, some gang activities certainly are because they often involve violence, carrying and using weapons, and theft.

- **Boredom** – some offenders commit offences because the risks involved give them a buzz and make their lives more interesting.
- **Psychological** – kleptomania is a recognised condition that compels people to steal. Others may commit offences because of anger or other emotions that they find difficult to control.

Activities

1 List the five reasons why people commit crime. Add to the list any other causes of crime you can think of. You can discuss this with a partner if you wish.

2 Using your list, put the causes in order, with the cause that you think is the hardest to deal with first and the easiest to deal with last.

3 'If offenders have a good reason for committing their offence, their punishment should be less severe'. What do you think? Explain your opinion.

The effects of crime

There is no such thing as a crime without a victim. Shoplifting increases the price we all pay for goods, car crime results in the victim making an insurance claim and this increases insurance premiums for others, and crimes of violence affect not only the victim but also their family and friends and medical staff who may have to give treatment. Police officers have the difficult and often dangerous task of dealing with the after-effects of crime, including arresting some of the most dangerous members of society. Some police officers lose their lives fighting crime, while others face serious injury, their lives being saved only by the protective clothing they are obliged to wear.

In addition to the personal and financial cost to the victims of crime, the whole of society suffers from the effects of crime.

- Many people are afraid to leave their homes at night for fear of being attacked or because they feel intimidated by groups of people.
- There is often a lack of trust between people in their everyday life or business dealings caused by the fear of dishonesty.
- The massive increase in CCTV in public areas and buildings has led to some fearing that their civil liberties and privacy are under threat. If there was less crime, there would be fewer cameras.
- Many people prefer to live in a society in which moral or religious values are upheld. The existence of crime threatens such values.

C   *Car crime affects more than just the owner of the car*

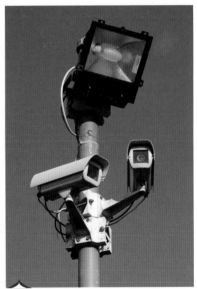
D   *Less crime would mean fewer cameras needed*

Activities

4 Do you agree that there is no such thing as a crime without a victim? Give reasons for your opinion.

5 Who are the victims of the crime in Photograph C?

6 Do you think that CCTV threatens civil liberties and privacy? Give your reasons.

Extension activity

Try to describe a society in which moral and religious values are upheld. Give some examples.

Summary

You should now understand some of the causes of crime and have thought about how crime affects the individual and society.

5.3 Punishment and forgiveness

Punishment

In Jewish thinking, the first recorded **punishment** comes in Genesis 3. God, having found out Adam and Eve had fallen to the temptation of the serpent and eaten the fruit from 'the tree of knowledge of good and evil', punished the serpent, then Eve and finally, Adam. However, despite the severity of the punishment, God showed mercy in making garments for them to wear before banishing them from the Garden of Eden.

God's mercy was also shown in the story of Noah. The punishment for the rest of mankind was terrible but Noah deserved justice and mercy for remaining with God and so was saved. This can also be interpreted as God saving the whole of the human race to serve him and the planet he created.

The laws in the Torah often state clearly which punishments should be given to offenders. Although at the time they were considered to be more than reasonable, nowadays many people interpret them as being harsh. The punishments did, however, introduce the idea of personal responsibility – if a person committed a crime, they were punished rather than their families and communities being punished as sometimes happened previously. This idea of personal responsibility is shown in Exodus:

Beliefs and teachings

But if there is serious injury, you are to take life for life, eye for eye, tooth for tooth, hand for hand, foot for foot.

Exodus 21:23–24

This is often quoted to reinforce a desire for harsh punishment out of revenge, but the idea of personal responsibility it implies made it an advance on previous ideas about punishment. Previously, if a crime was committed against one person, punishment often resulted in a whole family or tribe being killed. Under the new law, only the offender lost their life.

The Talmud later interprets this quotation as paying money to provide fair compensation for a wrong that has been done rather than a physical punishment.

Objectives

Investigate the concept of punishment.

Link punishment to forgiveness.

Key terms

Punishment: that which is done to people because they have broken the law.

Forgiveness: to pardon people for something that they have done wrong. In Biblical times, it is believed that only God could forgive sins.

Beliefs and teachings

An enemy will overrun the land;

he will pull down your strongholds

and plunder your fortresses …

I gave you empty stomachs in every city

and lack of bread in every town,

yet you have not returned to me, declares the Lord.

Amos 3:11 and 4:6–7

A *Adam and Eve disobeyed God and were punished*

Discussion activity

With a partner, discuss whether Exodus 21:23–24 should be interpreted as revenge, personal responsibility or fair compensation. Be prepared to share your ideas with others.

Throughout the Tenakh, whenever the Jews, or the Hebrews as they were previously known, suffered, there was a feeling that God was allowing other nations to defeat them in battle and to incorporate them into their empires or for natural disasters such as drought to befall them. However, they were never completely destroyed as a people. This idea of punishment is a theme of many of the prophets.

However, the underlying principle behind punishment is that it should promote and uphold justice – a key theme in the whole of Judaism. The Torah instructed the Hebrews to:

Beliefs and teachings

Appoint judges and officials for each of your tribes in every town the Lord your God is giving you, and they shall judge the people fairly. Do not pervert justice or show partiality ... Follow justice and justice alone.

Deuteronomy 16:18–20

Forgiveness

Whenever the prophets interpreted defeat in battle or natural disasters as punishment from God, they also carried a message of hope that God would not forget them but allow them to restore their covenant with him.

Beliefs and teachings

Come, let us return to the Lord.

He has torn us in pieces but he will heal us;

he has injured us but he will bind up our wounds.

After two days he will revive us;

on the third day he will restore us,

that we may live in his presence.

Hosea 6:1–2

Jews are taught that if they repent they will receive God's **forgiveness**. This idea is best seen in the annual festival of Yom Kippur (Day of Atonement), when it is believed that God makes the final decision about what will happen to each individual in the coming year. Those who have properly expressed sorrow for their sin (repentance) will be forgiven by God and granted a happy new year. The preceding days between Rosh Hashanah and Yom Kippur are used by Jews to seek forgiveness from people they have wronged throughout the previous year. Only when they have mended relationships between themselves and those they have wronged, can Jews honestly seek God's forgiveness.

Forgiveness does not mean a lack of punishment however. It is also a sign of personal strength and not weakness. Punishment is important for many reasons and it is seen as right to punish as well as forgive. Acceptance of punishment is a step on the path to repentance and therefore important.

Activities

4 Explain how the quotation from Hosea relates to forgiveness.
5 Why do you think that Yom Kippur is the most sacred day of the Jewish year?
6 Do you think that forgiveness is a sign of strength or a weakness? Explain your reasons.

Activities

1 From what you have read, explain how mercy is shown in punishments in the Tenakh.
2 What does the fact that the Hebrews were never completely destroyed as a people teach you about God's relationship with them?
3 Why do you think that the Hebrews were instructed to appoint judges in every town?

Extension activity

In your opinion, should punishment promote and uphold justice? Give your reasons.

B *A tallit and shofar are used in the synagogue at Yom Kippur*

Research activity

Find out more about Yom Kippur by doing a search at www.bbc.co.uk/religion

AQA Examiner's tip

Remember that forgiveness is not a replacement for punishment.

Summary

You should now understand the concept of punishment and be able to link it to forgiveness.

What does punishment achieve?

If the law is respected, it allows people to live their lives in a society that does not allow people to be exploited or to live in fear. It also ensures that a person can live in safety and protects their property. However, whenever there is a system of law in place, it has to be supported by a system of punishments. This allows the lawmakers to use the legal system to punish the lawbreakers on behalf of the rest of society. Without the threat of punishment, there would be less incentive for some people to keep the law.

Imagine there was no punishment for disturbing learning in school. Those who do not want their learning disturbed so they can work hard and earn good qualifications would possibly not be able to do so because of the behaviour of others. This would not be fair on them. Those who do not appreciate the opportunity to learn in school and do not value the importance of earning good qualifications would perhaps have less reason to behave well if they knew they would not be punished. In a sense, such people are punishing themselves by not achieving, but they are also punishing those who want to achieve but are prevented from doing so.

Objectives

Understand what punishment is trying to achieve.

Evaluate deterrence and reparation as aims of punishment.

A Punishments help people to respect the law

Activities

1. In your opinion, what is the purpose of punishment? Give evidence to support your opinion.
2. Explain how punishments for disturbing learning helps to reinforce the importance of learning.
3. If there was no punishment for disturbing learning, do you think it would be more difficult to learn in your school? Give your reasons.

AQA Examiner's tip

When evaluating how effective punishments are, it is important to remember the aims of such punishments.

Deterrence

Deterrence means to persuade people to keep the law by showing them what will happen to them, or others, if they break the law. If they see that burgling somebody's home will probably lead to them spending time in prison, they may be deterred from burglary because they don't want to go to prison. They may have been in prison before and the experience of being locked in a cell for most of the day with no freedom to do what they want to do might mean that they do not want to return there. This is a very powerful aim because it uses likely punishments as a way of persuading people to keep the law. This works with people who have been punished before and also with other people who haven't, but are aware of what happens to lawbreakers and don't want it to happen to them.

Key terms

Deterrence: to put people off committing crimes. One of the aims of punishment.

Reparation: if criminals commit a crime and are caught, their punishment should make up for the loss that the victim suffered as a result of that crime.

Judaism takes this aim very seriously. Jews focus on the history recorded in the Tenakh, which shows them what will happen if they go against the will of God. The terrible suffering the Jews endured in the Holocaust, although completely unjust, shows them what can happen to them or anybody else. In addition, Jews want to live in an orderly society where the law of God is respected so anything that helps to bring that about is welcomed. Although punishment should be humane, it becomes an example for others to learn from.

B

Reparation

Reparation means to pay something back. In the context of punishment, it means that an offender's punishment should allow them to pay something back to the society they have wronged. On an individual level, this is likely to be related to less serious crimes through service to the wronged community, although after the Second World War, Israel was successful in obtaining reparation from Germany (in the form of payment to the Israeli Government and to the World Jewish Congress) for the way Jews were treated in the Holocaust – one of the most serious crimes the world has ever witnessed.

Summary

You should now have thought about the purpose of punishment with the examples of deterrence and reparation.

Discussion activity

Spend 5 minutes discussing with a partner whether punishing people by making an example of them is wrong.

Activities

4 Explain the theory of how deterrence works.

5 What do you think Jews have learned from the sufferings they have endured? Give some examples.

Activity

6 Explain, using examples, what is meant by reparation as an aim of punishment

C *Cleaning graffiti off walls could be seen as reparation*

Aims of punishment (2) – protection, reformation, retribution and vindication

Protection

Any government has the responsibility to provide **protection** for their citizens and to allow them to live in a society where law and order are upheld. For this reason, serious offenders are taken out of society and put into prison to prevent them from causing further harm by committing further offences. Protection and deterrence are linked because deterring offenders from committing further crimes is also a way of protecting the rest of society. This can refer to any offences, not just the most serious.

Reformation

For many people, **reformation** is an important aim of punishment because it recognises that punishment should have a positive effect on the offender. While being punished, prisoners are helped to come to terms with the offence they have committed and see that it is wrong because it has caused harm to others, in the hope that when the punishment is finished, they will not want to reoffend. If the offender does not reoffend, society is protected by the fact the offender is reformed. The prophet Ezekiel reinforced this idea:

Beliefs and teachings

I take no pleasure in the death of the wicked, but rather that they turn from their wicked ways and live. Turn! Turn from your evil ways.

Ezekiel 33:11

In Britain, prisoners are offered opportunities for education, skill training and drug programmes, and so on, to help them to reform. In many countries, including Israel and Britain, if the authorities are satisfied that an offender is reformed, they may be released from prison early on parole. Behaving well in prison is taken as a sign that an offender is reformed.

Retribution

The word 'retribution' means to take revenge on an offender because they have committed an offence. Many people quote 'an eye for an eye, a tooth for a tooth' (Exodus 21:24) as evidence that retribution is the most important aim of punishment in Judaism.

This is an interpretation that the Talmud and Jews throughout the ages have denied. They point to other parts of the Torah, which give a more accurate picture:

Objectives

Know and understand four more aims of punishment.

Evaluate the effectiveness of these aims of punishment.

Key terms

Protection: to stop the criminal hurting anyone in society. An aim of punishment.

Reformation: punishment with the aim of changing the person's criminal behaviour and making them into a responsible citizen.

Retribution: if people do something wrong then they should receive a punishment that is fitting for the crime that they committed. Often referred to as revenge.

A *Reformation involves making the right choice of which way to go*

AQA Examiner's tip

You may see retribution referred to as revenge. You can use this if you wish to but it is probably best to use the term the examination paper may use, that is, retribution.

Retribution is a natural emotion but a harmful one. Punishments based on retribution tend to be harsh but they do serve to deter others and protect society.

Vindication

This is a very important aim of punishment for Jews. Vindication means to show that decisions or actions are correct. Therefore, punishment of offenders vindicates the law and shows society that the law is right and just. In Jewish law, this is especially important because of the Jewish belief that their law comes from God and therefore must be correct. Breaking God's law is more serious than breaking state law and punishments must reinforce this.

links

See pages 102–103 for more about the meaning of Exodus 21:23–24

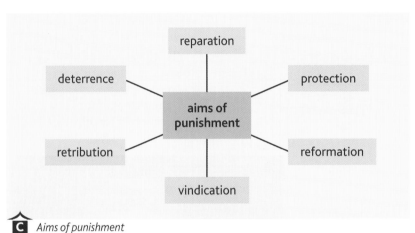

C   *Aims of punishment*

B   *Society is protected from this offender while he is in prison*

Summary

You should now know and be able to evaluate four further aims of punishment.

Types of punishment

Different types of punishment

British law has a massive range of punishments ranging from a caution to life imprisonment. A caution is given by the police and if an offender accepts the caution, it is recorded and no further action is taken. Some other criminal cases are judged by a local Magistrates' court, if the offence is not considered serious. Magistrates are volunteers from the community who, after training, make judgements and pass sentences including a short prison sentence, if they deem it appropriate and it is within the legal guidelines they have to follow. More serious cases are dealt with by the Crown Court, in front of a full-time judge who is an expert in the law and a jury of 12 adults drawn at random from the community. The jury listen to the evidence, take legal advice from the judge and decide whether the defendant is guilty or not. If the jury return a guilty verdict, the judge passes sentence. Judges are allowed to use the full range of punishments, although they have to obey guidelines issued by Parliament.

Objectives

Investigate different types of punishment.

Evaluate the use and worth of different types of punishment.

Discussion activity

With a partner, discuss whether you think that using a jury of 12 ordinary people is the best way to decide a person's guilt.

Key terms

Fine: a form of punishment in which an offender pays a sum of money.

Community service: work which helps the community – sometimes used as a punishment for offenders.

Activities

1 Briefly explain the British system of punishing offenders.
2 'Magistrates should not be allowed to put people in prison.' What do you think? Explain your opinion.

Fines

Fines for criminal offences can be given by any British court after the defendant has been found guilty. A Magistrates' court can fine a person between £200 and £5000; a Crown Court has no limits. In addition, fixed penalty notices can be imposed for such offences as illegal parking, speeding, graffiti and public disorder. These have to be paid to the Magistrates' court without the case being heard and judged and do not affect a person's criminal record. More serious offences carry a higher fine and the offender's ability to pay should be taken into account.

Community service

For offences that are considered to be quite serious and more serious than those for which a fine is given, a magistrate may decide to impose a period of unpaid **community service** of up to 300 hours. This may involve tidying up local beauty spots, working in a charity shop or removing graffiti.

Community service is considered appropriate for people whose crimes have harmed a community, such as being drunk and disorderly, committing anti-social behaviour or criminal damage. It can also be used for serious one-off offences such as driving while drunk or without a licence. The community work is closely supervised.

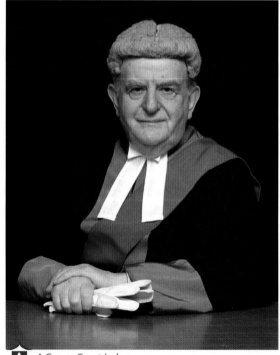

A A Crown Court judge

AQA Examiner's tip

If explaining what a particular punishment is, it will be helpful to give an example of an offence it may be used for.

B *Community service involves doing unpaid work in the community under close supervision*

Imprisonment

Imprisonment is the strongest type of punishment a British court can impose. Murderers and violent sex offenders have to be sentenced to life in prison and will usually serve at least 12 years before being considered for parole (early release from prison is possible if officials believe the offender is reformed), although some mass murderers and serial violent rapists will never be considered for parole. While in prison life may be more comfortable than some people believe it should be, the loss of freedom for a period of time and living in a heavily guarded institution with some of the most violent people in society is certainly not the 'holiday camp' some people accuse it of being. Indeed, the punishment is the loss of freedom, not any loss of the right to be treated in a humane fashion. Parole gives prisoners hope of early release and encourages them to show that they have reformed. It also encourages them to keep out of trouble while they are in prison.

There is no facility in British law for the **death penalty** to be imposed on any offender and corporal punishment (causing physical harm by beating, flogging, and so on) is not permitted.

Key terms

Imprisonment: when a person is put in jail for committing a crime.

Death penalty: form of punishment in which a prisoner is put to death for crimes committed.

Research activity

For more information about the criminal justice system in England and Wales look at **www.cjsonline.org**

Activities

3 Explain fines, community service and imprisonment.
4 Do you think that prisoners should be given parole? Explain your reasons.
5 Should murderers automatically be sent to prison for life? Give reasons for your answer.

Extension activity

Should people who have committed the same offence be fined different amounts only because one is more able to pay than the other? Explain your reasons.

Summary

You should now know about and have evaluated fines, community service and imprisonment as types of punishment.

The impact of punishment

Introduction

If a fellow student was told they were going to be punished for disturbing your learning and were secretly let off, you would probably be quite unhappy if you found out, because without punishment, there would be a good chance that it would happen again.

Even though most people accept that punishment is necessary and inevitable, nobody likes to be punished. Punishment is usually unpleasant, partly because its effect on the individual is demanded by those in society who want to ensure that it happens.

Impact on society

Punishment has a big impact on society. This could be a positive impact or a negative one.

- If offenders are encouraged not to reoffend or are taken out of society in order to go to prison, society is protected.
- Fines paid to a court help to provide finance for the government and is used for the benefit of the rest of society.
- Community service gives offenders the opportunity to make a positive contribution to society.
- Punishment reinforces a strong code of ethics – those that offend against a code of ethics are punished. This makes the code of ethics appear more important.
- Offenders put in prison leave behind families who are likely to need support, both financial and emotional.
- Imprisonment is very expensive – it costs anything between £30,000 and £40,000 per year to keep an offender in prison.
- Fines may result in families being short of money and community service may result in an offender losing their job.

Impact on the individual

Punishment affects different people in different ways. While offenders may be seen to be getting what they deserve, their families may feel as though they are being punished as well. However, in some cases, imprisonment may benefit others in a family.

The offender

- Many offenders find it difficult to cope in prison. If their offences involve children, other prisoners may react badly to them. Suicide is a major potential problem. Between 1978 and 2003, 1312 prisoners committed suicide in British jails.
- Some offenders have serious mental problems that imprisonment does not address and possibly makes worse.
- Addicts can receive help to combat their addiction while in prison.
- Community service can be embarrassing, especially where it is in full view of the public.

A Punishment can have both positive and negative impacts on society

Discussion activity

Spend a couple of minutes discussing with a partner whether punishment is necessary and inevitable. Can you think of circumstances where it isn't?

AQA Examiner's tip

If you are asked to explain ways that punishment has an impact on the individual and society, you only need to choose two or three to explain.

Life is different now that dad's in prison. Mum misses him most of the time but we are both glad he can't come in drunk most nights as he used to.

Mum was sent to prison and as dad didn't want me, I now live with Mary and Peter, my foster parents. They're great but I do miss my mum. I hope they'll let her out soon.

Mum has to do this community service thing. She used to work in a shop before the trial but she doesn't now. The shopkeeper said he couldn't afford to pay her but I think it is because of the community service.

■ There have been instances when non-guilty people are found guilty and punished by mistake.

■ Although many reoffend when released from prison, punishment may bring about real change in the future.

The offender's family

■ Children may react badly to one or both of their parents being taken out of the home and could be teased or bullied by their peers.

■ Removal of a wage earner will possibly mean that the family have to rely on state benefits, which may not be enough to maintain their standard of living.

■ Travelling to visit spouses, partners or parents in prison can be very expensive.

■ Children may be taken into care if parents are imprisoned. This splits up the family – the main unit in Jewish society.

■ If the parent, spouse or partner is being punished for domestic violence, removal of the offender will make their victims safe.

These are just some examples of the effect that punishment has on both offenders and their families. Most are negative but some are positive and helpful. You may be able to think of some more points that could be included.

C   *A parent being punished can have a huge effect on children*

Beliefs and teachings

The value of punishment as a deterrent and for the protection of society is widely recognized. But all the stress today is on the reformatory aspects of punishment. Against such a background, the whole question of reward and punishment in the theological sphere is approached in a more questioning spirit.

Rabbi Louis Jacobs

Activities

1   Who do you think *benefits* most from punishment – society, the offender or the offender's family? Explain your reasons.

2   Who do you think *suffers* most from punishment – society, the offender or the offender's family? Explain your reasons.

3   'An offender's children should be considered when their parent(s) are being sentenced' Do you agree? Explain your reasons.

Extension activity

Choose one of the three 'talking heads'. Write them a letter giving them some advice that you think may be helpful. Remember to be sensitive to their feelings.

Summary

You should now understand that punishment has an impact on society, the offender and their family and have evaluated this impact.

The death penalty

The **death penalty** is also known as capital punishment or execution. It was abolished in Britain in 1965 on a temporary basis, then permanently in 1969. It is now banned in many countries, including all those within the European Union. In some other countries, including Israel, it is still permitted but rarely or never used.

However, in other countries, including China and some states in the USA who have voted to keep it, the death penalty allows offenders found guilty of certain serious offences to be legally put to death. This can be by lethal injection or the electric chair, as in some states in the USA, or hanging, stoning or being shot in some other parts of the world. The US state of Texas executed 431 people between 1982 and 2009. There are currently 372 men and 9 women currently on 'death row' awaiting execution.

Objectives

Understand and evaluate arguments for and against the death penalty.

Key terms

Death penalty: form of punishment in which a prisoner is put to death for crimes committed.

Case study

On 11 February 2009, Wayne Tompkins was executed in Florida USA for killing Lisa De Carr, the 15-year-old daughter of his girlfriend. Lisa was reported missing by her mother on 24 March 1983. Tompkins admitted having spent much of the day with Lisa but claimed that she had run away. It was later alleged that Tompkins had sexually assaulted her before killing her. He was also accused of committing robbery and sexual assaults on two other women in April and May of 1984.

Lisa's body was found buried in a shallow grave under her house on 5 June 1984 and she was identified using dental records. However, the dental records were incomplete and several people signed sworn statements to the authorities saying that they had seen Lisa alive after her alleged murder took place. Despite this, Wayne Tompkins was found guilty of her murder in 1986 and sentenced to death.

The verdict was challenged in the courts and appeals to overturn the death penalty were made. Eventually, 23 years after having been found guilty of Lisa's murder and sentenced to death, Wayne Tompkins was executed.

Activity

1. Spend a whole minute silently thinking about the figures relating to the state of Texas and then write down five words that express your feelings about them.

Discussion activity

Using the information in the case study, decide whether you think that Wayne Tompkins should have been executed. Give your reasons and be prepared to share them with others.

Should the death penalty exist?

A An electric chair

AQA Examiner's tip

You can refer to examples in your exam if it is relevant, but don't spend a lot of time giving the details of the cases.

There are many arguments for and against the existence of the death penalty, based on religious and secular principles. Some think that murderers and terrorists forfeit the right to live when they commit their terrible crimes and that such people are not deserving of having money spent on keeping them in prison – the world would be a better place without them. People who think this also tend to interpret the quotation 'an eye for an eye, a tooth for a tooth' (Exodus 21:24) to mean that murderers should be killed and quote the sixth commandment 'You shall not murder' (Deuteronomy 20:13). They believe that society should be allowed to take revenge on murderers and that this would deter others and protect society.

CO links

For Jewish attitudes to capital punishment, see pages 114–115.

B   Can a jury ever be 100 per cent certain?

C   The last men executed in Britain were Peter Anthony Allen at Liverpool and Gwynne Owen Evans at Manchester on 13 August 1964

Others question whether society has the right to take somebody's life and point to cases where innocent people have been executed by mistake. Juries are supposed to have no reasonable doubt about whether the defendant is guilty or not, but they cannot be 100 per cent certain. The prospect of indirectly being responsible for the defendant's death may make some jurors reluctant to pronounce them guilty. Opponents of capital punishment may believe that reformation is more civilised than retribution and question whether capital punishment is a deterrent. As many people who murder have been diagnosed with either temporary or permanent psychological problems, it is claimed that it is preferable to treat them rather than kill them. In addition, it is believed that the executioner becomes no better than the murderer they are executing, when an execution takes place.

Activities

2   Using the information above and any of your own ideas write a paragraph in favour of the death penalty and one against.

3   Which of your two paragraphs did you find easiest to write? Explain why.

Extension activity

Do you think that the state should have the right to take a person's life? Give your reasons. Try to use the aims of punishment in part of your answer.

Summary

You should now understand and have evaluated attitudes to the death penalty.

Teachings of the Torah about punishment

Teachings on the death penalty

It is an inescapable fact that throughout the Torah, there are many offences that were said to be punishable by death. Thirty-six offences have been identified, ranging from murder and improper sexual relations to idol worship and incorrect observance of Shabbat.

> ### Beliefs and teachings
>
> Whoever sheds the blood of man, by man shall his blood be shed; for in the image of God has God made man.
>
> *Genesis* 9:6
>
> Anyone who curses his father or mother must be put to death.
>
> *Exodus* 21:17

Objectives

Understand and apply teachings of the Torah to punishment.

Consider the idea of reward as an alternative interpretation of the Torah.

However, these punishments can be seen as a reflection of the times in which they were proposed and in truth, for the last 2,000 years or more, the death penalty has been used very little in Jewish society.

The Talmud commentary on the Torah, written by Rabbis from around 200 CE and recording the oral law which had been established over preceding centuries, makes it virtually impossible to use the death penalty. According to the earliest component of the Talmud, the Mishnah, 23 judges had to be involved in a case where the death penalty was required. They also:

- emphasised the ideas of the sanctity of life and the instruction not to kill
- applied interpretations of texts in a strict way, which made them virtually impossible to use
- found alternative ways of punishing people, including paying compensation
- imposed rules of evidence, such as requiring at least two witnesses to testify not only that they had witnessed the crime but warned the offender of the potential consequence before the crime was committed. The offender had to say he accepted the warning in full knowledge of the consequences. His own confession of guilt could not be accepted.

In present day Israel, the death penalty was abolished in 1954, except for those convicted of Nazi war crimes. Even though several Nazi war criminals have been hunted down and convicted, only one – Adolf Eichmann, who had particular responsibility for the Holocaust – has been executed. After a four-month trial during which he claimed he was only obeying orders, he was found guilty and hanged at Ramleh Prison on 31 May 1962.

A *Adolf Eichmann visited Auschwitz concentration camp several times and witnessed the process of extermination there, that was being carried out as part of his 'final solution'*

Beliefs and teachings

A Sanhedrin (High Court) that executes a person once in seven years is a murderous one. Rabbi Eleazar ben Azariah said: 'Once in seventy years.' Rabbis Tarfon and Akiva said, 'If we were members of a Sanhedrin, nobody would ever be put to death.' Rabbi Simeon ben Gamliel dissented: '[If so, you] would [thus] multiply shedders of blood in Israel.'

Mishnah Makkot 1:10

To ensure a fair trial the rabbinic judges would ask: They would examine them with seven searching queries: In what seven-year period {did it take place}? In what year? In what month? On which day of the month? On what day of the week? At what hour? And, at what place? Did you know him?

Babylonian Talmud: Sanhedrin 40a

■ Other teachings

The focus of the Torah should not just be seen as threatening punishments for people who break God's law. The stories of Noah being saved from God's destruction, of Abraham being rewarded with a son because he stayed with the Lord, and of the Hebrews being taken from slavery to a new life in the 'promised land' should indicate that God is a God of love who will reward the faithful. Cain, the first born of Adam and Eve, was asked by God:

Beliefs and teachings

If you do what is right, will you not be accepted?

Genesis 4:7

and under the leadership of Moses, the Hebrews were told:

Beliefs and teachings

Be careful to follow every command I am giving you today, so that you may live and increase and may enter and possess the land that the Lord promised.

Deuteronomy 8:1

The emphasis is on using the freewill that God has given and choosing to obey the law for the promised reward and not because of the threat of punishment. This is a key theme that sometimes gets overlooked.

Most people respond best to reward and work hard to receive it. The threat of punishment is not relevant to them because they strive to do good and not bad. This is what the Torah allows and encourages Jews to do. It is not just a legalistic framework threatening punishment, but a liberating ethical guide to living in the way God wants his people to live with the promise of great reward for doing so in this life and eternally in the next. In addition, Jews are motivated to keep God's law by their desire to respond to God's love and care of them.

Activities

1   Explain Jewish teachings about the death penalty, including how the Talmud interprets the Torah.

2   Do you think that the rabbis who wrote the Talmud were correct in their interpretation of the Torah?

3   'Nazi war criminals should have faced the death penalty.' What do you think? Explain your opinion.

B   *The reward of following the Torah is a great one*

Activities

4   Explain how the Torah can be interpreted as offering reward rather than threatening punishment.

5   'Reward, not the threat of punishment, is better at encouraging people to use their freewill to behave well.' What do you think? Explain your opinion.

AQA   Examiner's tip

If evaluating the effectiveness of punishment, you can use the idea of reward motivating people to do good as an alternative opinion.

Summary

You should now understand and have applied teachings in the Torah to punishment and considered reward as an alternative interpretation.

5

Crime and punishment – summary

For the examination, you should now be able to:

✔ show understanding of how Jewish views of law, punishment and forgiveness influence attitudes to:

- aims of punishment including deterrence, protection, reformation, reparation, retribution and vindication
- types of punishment including fines, imprisonment, community service and the death penalty
- the impact of punishment on society and the individual
- the teaching of the Torah about punishment
- attitudes to forgiveness

✔ apply relevant Jewish teachings to each topic

✔ give your own opinions about each topic

✔ discuss topics from different points of view, including Jewish ones.

Sample answer

1 Write an answer to the following exam question:

Explain Jewish attitudes to the death penalty.

(6 marks)

2 Read the following answer:

> The Torah makes it quite clear that there are a lot of offences both criminal and religious that should be punished by the death penalty. As this is the law of God, you would expect that Jews would stick to it. However, rabbis about 2,000 years ago made it very difficult for courts to pass the death sentence on an offender. They said there must be 23 people involved in the decision and laws relating to witnesses were made almost impossible. This is because they thought that life was sacred and therefore nobody but God can take it away. Israel today does not allow the death sentence because of this.

3 With a partner, discuss the sample answer. Do you think that there are other things that the student could have included in the answer? Are there any inaccuracies here?

4 What mark would you give this answer out of six? Look at the mark scheme in the Introduction on page 7 (AO1). What are the reasons for the mark you have given?

AQA Examination-style questions

1   Look at the photograph below and answer the following questions.

(a)   Explain briefly two aims of punishment.   *(4 marks)*

 There is no need to explain more than two aims of punishment

(b)   Explain the Jewish beliefs about forgiveness.   *(4 marks)*

 Try to include teachings and examples in your explanation.

(c)   'The 613 mitzvoth should never be changed or broken.'
     Do you agree? Give reasons for your answer, showing that you have thought
     about more than one point of view. Refer to Judaism in your answer.   *(6 marks)*

 Make sure that you include two different points of view and reasons for each.

6.1 Jewish marriage

Marriage

Marriage is a social and legal contract made between a man and woman who commit to living together as husband and wife until death. In the UK, marriage is still the most popular form of living together and creating a new family. Many people believe that marriage is the first step in creating a stable environment in which to have and raise children. The contract of marriage also serves to protect and transfer property from one generation to the next. When a couple get married, in law they are recognised as a new family unit and are entitled to certain rights and privileges under the law. For example, they become the 'next of kin', which means that should either of them be in a position where they cannot make decisions for themselves, their marriage partner assumes that responsibility rather than their parents.

Jewish attitudes to marriage

In Judaism, marriage is called Kiddushin, which means dedication. It is more than just a social contract; it is the spiritual binding together of two people in love and commitment to each other. The Jewish teachings make clear that marriage is intended by God and is the natural state in which people should live. Through marriage, a number of positive things can be achieved.

The purpose of Jewish marriage

- To show commitment and love for each other in a lifelong binding agreement.
- To share sexual desires exclusively with one person in intimacy and dignity.
- To share companionship and support throughout life.
- To provide a secure foundation to have and raise children in a stable loving home.
- To share and grow spiritually in the faith and develop closeness to God.

> ### Beliefs and teachings
>
> He who finds a wife finds what is good and receives favour from the Lord.
>
> *Proverbs* 18:22
>
> A man will leave his father and his mother and will be united to his wife and they will become one flesh.
>
> *Genesis* 2:24
>
> One's love for God should parallel one's love for their spouse.
>
> *Maimonides*

> ### Objectives
> Know and understand Jewish attitudes to marriage.

> ### Key terms
> **Marriage:** a legal union between a man and a woman.

A For many, marriage is the start of a new family life

> ### Discussion activity
> In small groups, discuss the advantages and disadvantages of getting married. Why do you think that marriage is still a popular choice for many couples in the modern world? Share your views in a class debate.

B Jewish marriage ceremonies take place under a chuppah

Jewish marriage

The first step in any marriage is to find a suitable partner. Traditionally, Judaism teaches that finding a marriage partner should be based on intellect and emotion and not simply physical attraction. It has been customary for a close friend or relative to suggest a meeting between two people who they think may make suitable marriage partners. This is called shidduch or 'matchmaking'. Many Jewish people feel that it is important to have a Jewish partner for marriage as a child is seen to be Jewish if they have a Jewish mother. While it is not forbidden to marry a non-Jewish person, it can present difficulties that would not arise in an exclusively Jewish partnership.

Love and mutual attraction are important and ultimately a couple will decide for themselves if they wish to be married. When they reach this stage, the engagement will take place. The families will hold a small reception and make the announcement. Some choose to make a contract in which they agree the responsibilities of both families with regard to the completion of the marriage ceremony. For one week before the marriage ceremony, the couple will not see each other so that they enhance the joy experienced at the actual marriage ceremony. During this week, the bride and groom will also visit the mikveh (ritual bath) to ensure that they are ritually pure before the ceremony.

C *A Jewish marriage contract – Ketubah*

∞ links

For more on the mikveh, see pages 126–127.

Case study

A Jewish marriage ceremony

A Jewish marriage ceremony begins with the signing of the marriage contract called the Ketubah. This is a contract that details the husband's obligations to his wife, including food, shelter, pleasures and rights to his wealth should he die or divorce her. These obligations are usually written in illuminated scripts and are very beautiful. The contract is witnessed by two people and then the marriage service takes place.

The bride and groom stand under the chuppah (wedding canopy), which is a symbol of the new home they will be creating. The ceremony is led by a rabbi, who begins by reciting blessings over a cup of wine that the couple then share. The marriage contract is then read out and the groom places a ring on the third finger of the bride's left hand. The ring is plain and unbroken and symbolises the hope for a harmonious marriage.

The rabbi will then recite more blessings, including praise for God and thankfulness for joy and the happiness of the new couple. The groom then wraps the wine glass in cloth and breaks it with his foot. The glass breaking is a symbol of the sorrow of the Jewish people over the destruction of the temple in Jerusalem. So this is a reminder that even though they are present at a happy occasion, there would be more joy if they could fulfil the temple commandments. The couple then go to a private room to break their fast. The couple will share a meal before then rejoining their family and friends for celebrations.

Activities

1   What is a marriage?

2   Explain **three** reasons why some people choose to get married.

3   Explain Jewish attitudes to marriage. Refer to beliefs and teachings in your answer.

4   Explain some of the symbols used in a Jewish marriage ceremony.

5   'The most important reason for getting married is being in love.' Do you agree? Give reasons for your answer, showing that you have thought about more than one point of view. Refer to Judaism in your answer.

Summary

You should now know and understand Jewish attitudes to marriage and the purpose of marriage.

AQA Examiner's tip

Being able to refer to some of the symbols within the Jewish marriage ceremony will help you to show understanding of the purposes of marriage in Judaism.

Divorce

When people get married, they hope that it will be a lifelong commitment, but unfortunately people change and married life may not work out. In some cases, a couple may feel that the only way forward is to end their marriage. A **divorce** takes place when a couple seek a legal ending to their marriage. It can be a very difficult and traumatic time, not only for the couple, but for their family and friends. If they have children, it can be especially hard for them as they have to cope with the problems their parents are facing and the prospect of possibly not seeing one of them very often.

Why do people get divorced?

There is no simple answer to this. Often when a marriage ends in divorce, there will be a number of reasons. It also depends on the couple. Some divorces can be very amicable, with both people accepting that the marriage is over and just wanting to move on with their lives. Divorce can also get very bitter, especially if those involved feel that their partner has been cruel or unfair. In the UK, marriages can only be ended by going to law and seeking a legal dissolution of the marriage contract. In doing this, the couple have to give reasons for why they want a divorce.

Some marriages fail because people change and grow apart. Everyone is different and over time people develop new interests and aspirations their partners may not share. Sometimes the pressures of modern living can put strain on a marriage. For example, if one partner becomes unemployed or ill. Sometimes people meet someone else and feel that they would rather be with them than their spouse. Starting a family brings its own difficulties and challenges that may put pressure on a marriage. In some cases, couples find they have different ideas of how the marriage should develop. For example, one partner may want a family, the other may not. Whatever the reasons, divorce is never an easy option and all religious traditions encourage a couple to try to resolve their differences.

Jewish teaching about divorce

Marriage is very important in Judaism and so divorce is not generally seen as a good thing. If a couple are experiencing difficulties in their marriage, they should make every effort to resolve their differences and make the marriage work. However, Judaism accepts that sometimes this is not possible and permits a man to divorce his wife. No 'grounds', that is reasons, need to be given for a divorce.

Objectives

Understand why some people get divorced and consider Jewish teachings about divorce.

Key terms

Divorce: legal ending of a marriage.

Discussion activity ●●●

1   In small groups, discuss the reasons why marriages might fail. Do you think some of the reasons for obtaining a divorce are better than others? Should divorce be made more difficult to obtain?

A *A decree nisi ends a marriage*

Jewish teaching states only that in the case of adultery, divorce must take place, even if the man is prepared to forgive his wife for her sexual misconduct. Only the man can initiate a divorce under Jewish law.

Beliefs and teachings

You shall not commit adultery.

Exodus 20:14

If a man marries a woman who becomes displeasing to him because he finds something indecent about her and he writes her a certificate of divorce, gives it to her and sends her from his house …

Deuteronomy 24:1

Do not break faith with the wife of your youth. "I hate divorce," says the Lord.

Malachi 2:15 –16

The Get

The instruction in Deuteronomy is for a man to simply write his wife a bill of divorce and present this to her. This document is called a 'Get' and it confirms that a marriage is over and the woman is free to remarry if she chooses. However, because in ancient times this led to men divorcing their wives for trivial reasons like burning the dinner, the Jewish courts introduced specific laws and procedures to make sure that divorce was conducted fairly.

When a couple have agreed to divorce, they apply to the Jewish court (Bet Din) for a date to end their marriage. On the agreed date, the couple attend the court where a scribe will write out the Get for the husband in front of the judges. The husband will then hand the document to his wife in the presence of witnesses. This formally ends the marriage in Jewish law. It is not always necessary for the couple to have to go personally to the court, as this could be very difficult if the marriage has ended bitterly. In this case, they can send a representative, usually a family member or good friend to act on their behalf. Obtaining a Get only grants a divorce in religious terms. Unless a Jewish couple live in Israel, they must also seek a civil divorce through the legal procedures of the country in which they live. Otherwise, they will not be able to marry again if they so wish.

Activities

1. What is a divorce?
2. Explain three reasons why some marriages may end in divorce.
3. Explain how and why a Get is important for a Jewish couple who are divorcing.
4. 'Marriage should be for life.' Do you agree? Give reasons for your answer, showing that you have thought about more than one point of view. Refer to Judaism in your answer.

Summary

You should now know and understand some reasons why marriages may end in divorce. You should know and understand why a Get is important for Jewish couples who decide to divorce.

 links

Find the definition of the word 'adultery' in the Glossary at the back of this book.

Discussion activity

2. Discuss with a partner reasons why it is important for Jewish couples to obtain a Get.

links

See pages 122–123 for more on Jewish attitudes to divorce and remarriage.

 A Bet Din presides over the issuing of a Get

Research activity

Find out more about the ancient traditions related to marriage and divorce. How has Jewish practice and teaching developed in ensuring greater equality and rights for women?

Discussion activity

3. Find out more about the Jewish understanding of 'uncleanliness'. Write a short guide to what this means; you can include information that goes beyond the topic of marriage and divorce.

AQA Examiner's tip

When explaining reasons, giving examples to illustrate your point helps to show that you understand the issue.

Jewish attitudes to divorce

Jewish teachings have always allowed for the possibility of the marriage failing and there being a need for divorce. The marriage contract includes provision for the wife in case her husband should later divorce her. Judaism accepts that sometimes marriages do fail and that it is unhelpful to blame anyone for this because it will only add to the unhappiness and pain of the split. In Deuteronomy, a man is instructed simply to give his wife a bill of divorce and the marriage is over. In ancient times, this meant that a man could divorce his wife for any reason and she had to accept this.

In the 11th century, the Jewish courts made changes to the divorce laws to give greater protection to married women. In particular, the court ruled that a man can only divorce his wife with her consent and made provision for women to have the court act on their behalf if they wanted a divorce from an abusive or unfaithful husband. It is still the case that only a man can initiate a divorce under Jewish law.

Unless they live in Israel, Jewish couples who wish to divorce must use the courts of the country in which they live to obtain a legally recognised divorce. However, many feel it is still important to obtain a Get because without it, they are still considered to be married under Jewish law. This is especially important for the woman, should she remarry and have children. Without a Get, her marriage would be viewed as adultery and her children illegitimate. The Get is also important spiritually as it means that the Jewish laws have been fulfilled and the couple can continue in their faith knowing that they have not broken any of the commandments.

Jewish attitudes to remarriage

Remarriage describes the situation when a person who has been previously married, marries someone else. This may be because their partner has divorced them or passed away. In the event of death, remarriage does not present any problems because the marriage has not been ended deliberately. In the case of divorce, however, some would regard it as wrong to remarry because they believe that marriage should be a binding contract for life.

Judaism accepts remarriage as family life is a really important aspect of the Jewish lifestyle. If a couple were divorced when they were still quite young, especially if they did not have children, remarriage would be encouraged. However, there are restrictions on remarriage. A couple who have been divorced are forbidden from remarrying each other although they are permitted to marry someone else. A woman who has been divorced must have a Get in order to remarry; otherwise her marriage would be seen as adulterous. Men who are 'Kohen' (descended

Objectives

Understand Jewish attitudes to divorce and remarriage.

🔗 links

Find out more about the 'Get' on pages 120–121.

A   *Couples sometimes cannot get along*

Key terms

Remarriage: getting married again.

B   *Rabbis are forbidden to marry divorcees*

from the priestly classes) are also not allowed to remarry a divorcee. In the books of Ezra and Malachi, Jewish men who had married non-Jewish women were ordered to divorce them and marry Jewish women to preserve the Jewish nation.

Beliefs and teachings

Even God shares tears when anyone divorces his wife.

Talmud Sanhedrin 22a

After she leaves his house (her husband's) she becomes the wife of another man.

Deuteronomy 24:2

Rachael's story

My name is Rachael and I married my first husband when I was nineteen. We were very much in love at the time, but after a couple of years things started to get difficult. It came to a point where we were just arguing all the time and could not get along. We did go to counselling, but we decided that our marriage was over. I guess we were just too young. My husband divorced me and he also gave me a Get so that I could remarry in the future. This was really important to me because I very much wanted to have a family. I have been married to my second husband Ethan for 15 years and we have two children. We met a couple of years after my divorce at a family celebration. He was not concerned at all that I had been married before and having the Get meant that we could have a Jewish marriage ceremony. We are very happily married and have a wonderful family life.

C   *Rachael*

Case study

Discussion activity

Discuss in small groups why someone might wish to remarry when they have already failed to make one marriage work? Do you think that people should be allowed to marry more than once?

Activities

1. Explain Jewish attitudes to divorce.
2. 'Jewish couples should always try to avoid divorce.' What do you think? Explain your opinion.
3. What does Judaism teach about remarriage?
4. 'Religion should have nothing to do with marriage or divorce; it is a private matter for the two people concerned.' Do you agree? Give reasons for your answer, showing that you have thought about more than one point of view. Refer to Judaism in your answer.

links

Look up the meaning of the word 'divorcee' in the Glossary at the back of this book.

Summary

You should now know and understand Jewish attitudes to divorce and remarriage.

AQA   Examiner's tip

Using quotes or paraphrases from Jewish teachings will help to improve your answers.

Human sexuality

Judaism teaches that sex is a natural and enjoyable gift from God when it occurs within the loving relationship of a man and a woman who have committed to each other in marriage. Sex is an important part of this relationship not only for the purpose of having children, but as a sharing of companionship, love and intimacy. Jewish law recognises that there must be a physical attraction between couples who are to be married and forbids the forcing of marriage between two people who are not physically attracted. Sex should be a joyful act between couples and should not occur if a couple are quarrelling or drunk. The woman has a right to sex and her husband is instructed to be aware of her needs and ensure her pleasure. A wife should not deny her husband sexual relations and withholding herself from engaging in sexual intercourse can be a reason for divorce.

> ### Beliefs and teachings
>
> It is not good for man to be alone.
>
> *Genesis* 2:18
>
> David comforted his wife Bathsheba, and he went to her and lay with her.
>
> *2 Samuel* 12:24

Chastity

Chastity means not to engage in sexual activity and is often connected with the choice of an unmarried lifestyle, which is celibacy. Judaism teaches that chastity should be observed before marriage. However, the practice of deliberately choosing not to marry and have sexual relations is not considered to be a superior lifestyle to the married state, as it is in some other religious faiths. In Judaism it is expected that rabbis will be married, often before they have undergone their training. Judaism places great value and importance on the role of the family and it is expected that most people will find a suitable partner with whom they will enjoy a lifelong marital partnership. During a marriage, there will be periods of abstinence from sexual relations during the woman's period of menstruation and after childbirth. This time is called niddah and is a period or ritual impurity.

Sex outside marriage

Sex outside of marriage is generally regarded as wrong in Judaism, although the Torah does not actually forbid sexual intercourse between a consenting man and woman who are not married to anyone else. However, it does warn against promiscuity and wrongful sex acts. Jewish teachings also encourage couples to wait until marriage and a couple who are engaged should not be left without a chaperone for more than a short time. A chaperone is a responsible adult, usually a relative or family friend, who will accompany the couple when they meet.

When a couple are married, they make a commitment to be faithful to each other. To engage in sexual relations with anyone other than

Objectives

Understand Jewish attitudes to chastity, sex outside marriage and homosexuality.

A *Physical attraction is important between married couples*

∞ links

For more on the Jewish idea of ritual impurity, and the mikveh see pages 126–127.

Key terms

Chastity: refraining from sex outside of the married relationship.

Homosexuality: attraction to a member of the same gender.

Homosexual relationship: a sexual relationship with someone of the same sex.

a spouse is to commit adultery and is strictly forbidden. The Ten Commandments include a specific rule not to commit adultery and the 10th commandment also warns about desiring another man's wife. Committing adultery is a grave sin and in ancient times was even punishable by death. Marriage is the foundation of family life and an adulterous affair risks the security and happiness of everyone within that family. It is considered wrong that the Jewish law actually demands that a man divorces his wife if she is unfaithful to him.

Beliefs and teachings

A man who loves wisdom brings joy to his father, but a companion of prostitutes squanders his wealth.

Proverbs 29:3

A prostitute is a deep pit, and a wayward life a narrow well.

Proverbs 23:27

You shall not commit adultery.

Exodus 20:14

B *Some branches of Reform Judaism accept gay marriages*

Homosexuality

A **homosexual relationship** refers to a sexual relationship between two people of the same sex. The Torah makes clear that homosexual acts are forbidden and were even punishable by death at one time. In the book of Leviticus, Jewish women are told not to follow the ways of the Egyptians and Canaanites. This is believed to refer to the sexual practices of women marrying each other or a man marrying a woman and her daughter. Orthodox Judaism, therefore, considers homosexual relationships to be wrong. However, some branches of Reform Judaism place emphasis on the loving relationship between two people and regard their conduct in private as between the two people involved. They also accept the validity of civil marriages between gay couples. Reconstructionist Judaism, a group developed from Reform Judaism, places emphasis on the equality of all people; it permits homosexuals to be rabbis and will marry gay couples in a religious service.

As we celebrate the love between heterosexual couples, so too we celebrate the love between gay or lesbian Jews.

1992 Report of the Reconstructionist Commission on Homosexuality

Beliefs and teachings

Do not lie with a man, as one lies with a woman; that is detestable.

Leviticus 18:22

The cities of Sodom and Gomorrah were believed to be destroyed because of immoral sexual conduct.

Genesis 19

Discussion activity

'Homosexual couples should have the same rights as heterosexual couples.' Prepare arguments for and against this statement and then hold a class debate.

AQA Examiner's tip

Being able to show an awareness of different attitudes within Judaism to some issues demonstrates a deeper understanding of the topic.

Activities

1   What does Judaism teach about sex?
2   Explain why chastity is not considered to be a suitable lifestyle in Judaism.
3   What is adultery? Explain two reasons why it is considered wrong in Judaism.
4   Explain differing Jewish attitudes to homosexuality.
5   'Religion should not try to control human sexuality.' How far do you agree? Give reasons for your answer, showing that you have thought about more than one point of view. Refer to Judaism in your answer.

Summary

You should now know and understand Jewish attitudes to chastity, sex outside marriage and homosexuality.

The mikveh

What is a mikveh?

A **mikveh** is a special pool or bath designed for **ritual cleansing**. It is particularly important for Orthodox Jews, who observe all of the ancient mitzvoth recorded in the scriptures. Ritual cleansing means to wash away impurities and become ritually pure. Many of the rules of worship and family life cannot be conducted if a person is in a state of uncleanliness according to Jewish tradition. This includes things such as touching a corpse, menstruation or if a man has had a night emission of semen. In ancient times, the mikveh was so important that when a new Jewish community formed, Jews would build this before building a synagogue.

Mikveh means a collection of water and it is possible for a river or lake to be used as a mikveh. However, this is not always practical and so there is a need for a specially built mikveh within Jewish communities. The building must be designed to allow for the immersion pool to be connected to a natural collection of rain water and the pool itself must be big enough for a person to be completely covered by the water. There will be separate showers and changing rooms for men and women, which are used to prepare for their immersion. It is important to remember that the use of the mikveh is not to do with being physically clean; it is a spiritual cleansing that is occurring.

Key terms

Mikveh: a ritual bath designed for the total immersion of people so that they might be cleansed.

Ritual cleansing: when a person undergoes a purifying ceremony, e.g. a woman bathes in the mikveh at the end of menstruation.

A *Jewish men and women immerse themselves fully under the water to achieve ritual purity*

Use of the mikveh

There were many reasons why Jews in the past would visit the mikveh, especially before attending the temple to offer sacrifices. Today, however, the use of the mikveh is much less common. It is mostly used by Orthodox women who will attend once a month. Judaism teaches that a woman is unclean whilst she is menstruating and that during this time, there can be no sexual relations between her and her husband. This time is known as a woman's niddah, a period of ritual impurity. When her period finishes, she will go to the mikveh to wash away her impurity and may then resume an intimate relationship with her husband. They will also go after the birth of a baby and on the day before they get married.

Men also use the mikveh. Most men will attend the mikveh before they are married and every year on the eve of Yom Kippur (the holiest day in the Jewish calendar). Some may choose to go more frequently, for example, before Shabbat and other festivals, but this is not required. The mikveh is also used by people who wish to become Jews and it is a compulsory part of the initiation rituals into the faith.

Research activity

1 Find out more about Jewish teachings about cleanliness (purity) and uncleanliness (impurity).

Discussion activity

Discuss in small groups how Jewish teachings about cleanliness and uncleanliness may present problems for Jewish people living in a non-Jewish community.

A further feature of the mikveh design is the inclusion of a separate pool for the washing of new utensils intended for food preparation. Things like glasses, cups, plates, cutlery and saucepans must be washed and then cleansed of impurity in the mikveh before being used for the first time. The only exception is if it is known that the products have been made by a Jew and have not come into contact with non-Jews. This is to fulfil the mitzvoth connected with the Jewish food laws.

The immersion

When a person attends the mikveh, they will first prepare by removing all jewellery and make up as nothing must come between the body and the water. They will then shower and go to the immersion pool. There will be an attendant; male for men, female for women; who are there to ensure that the ritual is conducted properly. They will walk naked into the pool and immerse themselves fully under the water. When they come up, they will fold their arms and recite a blessing before again immersing themselves in the water. As they come up from the water this second time, they are now ritually pure again.

To outsiders, the use of the mikveh may seem strange. Certainly some of my non-Jewish friends think it must be very difficult not to touch my husband during my niddah, which are the days that I am menstruating and before I attend the mikveh. However, I explain to them that this is a very special time for us because we show our love for each other in other ways. It helps to remind us that our marriage is built on more than just our physical attraction.

B

 Converts to Judaism must be immersed in water before they can be accepted into the faith

Research activity

2 Find out about attitudes to the mikveh in Reform Judaism. Write a summary of your findings.

Activities

1 What is a mikveh and why is it important in Judaism?
2 Explain the use of the mikveh in Judaism.
3 'There is no need for a mikveh; the ritual could be performed at home.' What do you think? Explain your opinion.

Summary

You should now know that the mikveh has several different uses and understand Jewish teachings and attitudes to the mikveh.

Family life

A family is the basic social unit of all societies. A nuclear family is made up of parents and children. The extended family includes all other blood relations. The family plays an important role in governing human behaviour. Judaism teaches monogamy between couples and thus the family unit controls sexual behaviour. It is also the place where most people spend a great deal of their time. The family is where children are raised and learn social behaviour so that they may grow up and contribute positively to society. Within the family, there is also safety and security for the sick, disabled or elderly.

Objectives

Understand Jewish teachings about the roles and responsibilities of parents and children.

A   *A Jewish family celebrates Shabbat*

Beliefs and teachings

Honour your father and your mother.

Exodus 20:12

Children's children are a crown to the aged, and parents are the pride of their children.

Proverbs 17:6

He who spares the rod hates his son, but he who loves him is careful to discipline him.

Proverbs 13:24

The Shema

The Shema includes the instruction to teach children the word of God. Parents have a duty to teach their children their faith.

Deuteronomy 6:4–7

Research activity 🔍

Find out about the celebration of Shabbat in the family home. Write an account of the Shabbat celebrations and include an explanation of the roles of the family members in the celebration. Also include a summary of how Shabbat helps to strengthen Jewish family life.

Jewish attitudes to family life

The family is very important in Judaism and a great deal of Jewish practice is conducted in the home; for example, the keeping of Shabbat and kosher food laws as well as the celebration of festivals such as Passover and Sukkoth. Within the family, all members have important roles and responsibilities. As children grow up, parents are expected to teach them the customs and traditions of their faith and gradually the children take on more religious duties within the home.

Within a marriage, there are traditionally clearly defined roles for men and women. The roles of men and women are equal and complementary; they are intended to provide a firm and secure foundation for family life. Men are expected to work to provide for their wife and children and take responsibility for decisions within the home. Women are expected to look after the home and raise children. In the modern world, however, it is not uncommon for both parents to work and share the home responsibilities.

Parents are expected to nurture, love and care for their children. They are to set a good example to their children. Parents are expected to teach their children the beliefs and practices of Judaism and to guide them in understanding the mitzvoth (religious laws). When a male child is born, the parents are responsible for ensuring that they are entered into the covenant through the Brit Milah ceremony. They are also responsible for their children's religious duties until they come of age at Bar Mitzvah, which is 13, for boys and Bat Mitzvah, which is 12, for girls.

As children grow and develop, Jewish parents will teach them how to observe the Sabbath and other celebrations, how to keep a kosher kitchen and live a good Jewish life. Parents will often ensure that their children attend the synagogue and encourage them to participate in study and activities associated with their faith. On Friday evening, men will often attend worship in the synagogue while the women remain at home with the children and prepare to welcome Shabbat into the home.

Jewish children also have duties and responsibilities. They are expected to show respect for their parents and accept their guidance and discipline. As they grow up, they participate and take responsibility for observing some of the customs and traditions of their faith, for example, clearing the house of leaven at Passover and reciting some of the prayers. When a Jewish girl is Bat Mitzvah, she can take on the responsibility of welcoming in the Sabbath if her mother is unable to do this. When children become adults they are responsible for ensuring their elderly parents are cared for and may have them live with them in their family home.

B *Jewish children have religious duties and responsibilities*

What are legal drugs?

A drug is any substance that affects the mind or body. A legal drug is one that is not forbidden by the law. These will be used for medical and social reasons. When a drug is prescribed by a doctor, it is obviously intended to cure illness or alleviate pain. Few would object to the use of these drugs as the intention is good. Drugs such as alcohol and tobacco are also legal in the UK and are sold for adult use. These drugs are taken socially for pleasure. However, there are issues arising out of the use of these drugs because they can also have damaging effects on the individual, their families and society.

Jewish attitudes to legal drugs

Prescribed drugs

Judaism teaches that all people are made by God and that the body should be respected. There are a number of laws in Judaism that govern ritual purity, including the covenant of circumcision and the use of the mikveh. Leviticus 13 also includes many instructions for those with infectious diseases, who were regarded as ritually unclean. Caring for the body is therefore important. Judaism also teaches that God has given people the gift of intelligence and that it is right to use this to benefit humanity. Throughout life, most people are likely to be ill at some time and it is sensible to seek the advice of a doctor. It is acceptable for Jews to use drugs if the intention is to cure illness or relieve pain. **Prescribed drugs** and 'over the counter' medicines are therefore permitted.

A Prescribed drugs are not forbidden in Judaism

Tobacco

Tobacco is a legally available drug used by over 1 billion people worldwide. It can be smoked, chewed or sniffed. The tobacco industry is worth billions and is an important part of the economy of a number of economically developed and developing countries. It contains a substance called nicotine, which is very addictive. However, we now know that it is also extremely harmful. In the short term, tobacco has unpleasant effects on the user such as the smell, staining of hands and teeth, bad breath and poor skin. In the long term, smoking can lead to cancer, heart disease, emphysema and early death.

Objectives

Understand Jewish attitudes to the use of prescribed drugs and tobacco.

Key terms

Prescribed drugs: drugs which are legal, obtained on written instruction of a doctor.

Beliefs and teachings

The priest is to examine him, if the rash has spread in the skin, he shall pronounce him unclean, it is an infectious disease.

Leviticus 13:8

Elisha sent a messenger to say to him 'Go wash seven times in the Jordan and your flesh will be restored.'

2 Kings 5:10

B *Many countries in Europe have banned smoking in public places*

Judaism does not forbid the use of tobacco and it is a matter of conscience for each individual. Jewish connections with the tobacco trade in some countries meant that in the past many Jews did smoke or use snuff (a form of tobacco which is sniffed). It was widely believed that smoking actually had health benefits and some rabbis even engaged in a debate about whether or not a blessing should be recited before smoking because it was pleasurable in the same way as eating and drinking wine.

Today, the damaging effects of nicotine use are well known and consequently Judaism encourages people not to smoke. Judaism strictly forbids people from recklessly endangering their own bodies, which Jews say are created by God. Some would regard smoking as disrespectful to God. Those who do smoke are expected to try to give up and adults have a responsibility not to encourage children to smoke by doing this in front of them. Additionally, the effects of passive smoking mean that a Jew should not smoke around non-smokers because he or she is causing harm to them.

Beliefs and teachings

And God said 'Let us make man in our image, in our likeness.'

Genesis 1:26

Discussion activity

'Smoking should not be allowed in any public spaces inside or outside, so that children are not encouraged to take up the habit.' Discuss the advantages and disadvantages of this proposal in a small group. Share your ideas with the rest of the class and take a vote.

Research activity

Visit www.wikipedia.org. Search for 'Smoking in Jewish law' and find out more about the debate within Judaism regarding the use of tobacco.

Activities

1 What is a drug?
2 Explain Jewish attitudes to the use of prescribed drugs.
3 Explain changing Jewish attitudes to the use of tobacco.
4 'A Jew should never smoke.' What do you think? Explain your opinion.

Summary

You should now know and understand Jewish attitudes to the use of prescribed drugs and tobacco.

 Examiner's tip

When asked to explain attitudes, it is helpful to show that there are different attitudes to this issue and that Judaism indicates smoking is a matter of individual conscience.

Alcohol

Alcohol is a legal drug in most parts of the world. People have been fermenting wines, spirits and beers for centuries. For many people, alcohol is part of everyday life and in the UK many adults regularly drink at home and when out socialising. Alcohol is available from many sources including supermarkets, pubs, clubs and restaurants. Many people would probably say that there is nothing wrong with drinking in moderation.

Objectives

Understand Jewish attitudes to alcohol.

The effects of alcohol

People are affected by alcohol in different ways. Some people would say that they drink because they enjoy the effects of feeling happy and relaxed as well as the actual taste of the drink. However, alcohol has a depressant affect on the body. It slows down brain activity and reflexes; this is why people are more prone to having accidents when they are drunk. It can also cause personality changes.

A   Drinking is part of modern life for many young people

People can become more aggressive or less inhibited, leading them to do things they would not normally do. Long-term abuse of alcohol can lead to addition. Alcoholics are more likely to die from liver disease and the impact of their drinking on family life can be devastating.

Inability to work

Loss of self-control

Family breakdown

Addiction

Domestic violence

Criminal activity

Financial problems

Health problems

Loss of self-esteem

B   The possible effects of alcohol abuse

Jewish attitudes to alcohol

Judaism permits the drinking of alcohol in moderation and wine is used in a number of Jewish ceremonies and festivals. During Shabbat, the Kiddush blessing is recited over a cup of wine to mark the holiness of the day and then is shared by the family members. At birth and marriage ceremonies, wine is a symbol of joy and celebration. In the festival of Purim, the Talmud says that Jews should get drunk enough so that they do not know the difference between blessing Mordachai or cursing Haman (characters in the story of Esther told at Purim). Wine is accepted as a gift from God and there is nothing wrong with having a drink, providing alcohol is used responsibly.

C Judaism permits the drinking of alcohol in moderation

Beliefs and teachings

Wine is a mocker and beer a brawler; whoever is led astray by them is not wise.

Proverbs 20:1

Should I give up my wine which cheers both God and men?

Judges 9:13

There is no joy without wine since wine gladdens the heart of humanity.

The Talmud Pesahim 109A

When wine enters in sense goes out.

Midrash

You and your sons are not to drink wine or other fermented drink whenever you go into the Tent of meeting (worship).

Leviticus 10:9

Jewish teachings include warnings against the abuse of alcohol and several stories in the scriptures mention how alcohol can lead to destruction. For example, Noah was disgraced while under the influence of alcohol (Genesis 9:21) and Proverbs warns that drunkenness can lead to immoral acts. Some people interpret the tree of knowledge in the Garden of Eden as in fact being a grapevine, and consequently Adam and Eve's sin was brought about by being intoxicated. Judaism considers it wrong to use alcohol to avoid personal responsibilities and addiction to alcohol should be avoided.

 D Wine is used in many Jewish celebrations including Shabbat

Activities

1 Explain why some people drink alcohol.

2 Explain **three** reasons why alcohol abuse is wrong.

3 Explain the Jewish teaching about the use of alcohol.

4 'Drinking too much is always wrong.' Do you agree? Give reasons for your answer showing that you have thought about more than one point of view. Refer to Judaism in your answer.

Research activity 🔍

Find out about the use of wine in a number of Jewish celebrations. Write a guide explaining how and why wine is used and what it symbolises in these ceremonies and festivals.

AQA Examiner's tip

Some evaluation questions will be worth six marks. In these questions, you need to make sure that you give reasons that support more than one point of view

Summary

You should now know and understand Jewish attitudes to alcohol. You should know that alcohol is used in religious ceremonies and that Jews believe that alcohol should only be used in moderation.

Illegal drugs

What are illegal drugs?

Illegal drugs are those that are banned by the laws of a country. They are drugs considered to be especially harmful to the individual and to society. They include drugs such as heroine, ecstasy, cocaine, amphetamines and cannabis. In the UK, illegal drugs are classified according to their effects. Anyone found in possession of these drugs or trading them to others is committing a criminal offence. The fines and prison sentences can be very high, especially for those caught with class A drugs.

Why do people use illegal drugs?

People who use illegal drugs often do so for the same reasons that many people use legal social drugs. Having fun, enjoying the effects and being in a social environment are just some of the reasons that people give for using legal and illegal drugs. Among young people, drug-taking is often associated with peer pressure and the desire to rebel. Being part of a gang may well include an expectation that drugs will be used, for example, smoking cannabis. Some drugs are part of popular culture and some people see nothing wrong with experimenting and enjoy the effects of the drugs they take. However, many illegal drugs are highly addictive and it does not take long for the user to become dependent. When this happens, there can be devastating consequences.

Objectives

Understand Jewish attitudes to the use of illegal drugs.

Key terms

Illegal drugs: drugs whose possession is against the law.

Research activity

Find out more about the classification of illegal drugs. Do you think this is a good idea?

I smoke weed with my friends. Everyone does it and I don't want to be different.

I use drugs; they help me relax and have a good time at parties; they keep me going all night.

I have so much pressure at work; lots of debts and family problems; the drugs just help me forget all that for a while.

There's nothing to do round here. A friend suggested I try a hit and I liked the way it made me feel but now I'm addicted.

A

Discussion activity

Read the reasons the young people in the illustration give for using illegal drugs. Are any of the reasons the same as why people use alcohol? What other reasons can you think of as to why some people may use illegal drugs? What advice could you give to each of these young people about their drug use?

Jewish attitudes to illegal drugs

Judaism teaches that it is important to care for the body and mind. Life is a gift from God and is holy and valuable. This means that to do anything that deliberately destroys human life is wrong, including causing harm to oneself. Illegal drug use is therefore strictly forbidden in Judaism. God has provided people with a code to live by that involves keeping many religious laws. The purpose of this lifestyle is to draw the person into a closer relationship with God and to prepare them for the afterlife. It would be impossible to fulfil these religious duties and obligations under the influence of drugs. Anyone who does become dependent on drug use should be helped to overcome their addiction.

B   *Illegal drugs are a serious cause of crime in the UK*

Drug-taking is also seen as wrong because of its harmful effects on the family and society. Long-term drug use affects a person's personality and can make them violent and aggressive. It can also cause them to be unable to work and interact normally with other people. An addict will inevitably be very difficult to live with and this can put a family under a lot of strain. Family life is very important in Judaism and it would be very wrong for a person to bring such difficulties needlessly upon their family.

Judaism teaches that people should follow and respect the law. Possessing and dealing in illegal drugs is a crime and so no Jewish person should disgrace themselves or their families in this way. The affects of drug addiction on society are also a concern. Judaism teaches and encourages the establishment of harmonious societies where all people can live in peace. Drug use often leads to violence and criminal activity and innocent people are hurt. This is against the teachings of Judaism.

Activities

1   What are illegal drugs? Give examples in your answer.

2   Explain **three** reasons why some people use illegal drugs.

3   Explain Jewish attitudes to the use of illegal drugs.

4   'People should not use drugs for pleasure, even if they are legal drugs.' Do you agree? Give reasons for your answer, showing that you have thought about more than one point of view. Refer to Judaism in your answer.

Case study

A Jewish drug rehabilitation program

Torah and the Twelve Steps is an organisation that works with people who have become addicted to drugs or other problems, such as eating disorders and gambling. It aims to help Jewish people overcome their addiction by identifying the underlying reasons for their drug use. They regard addiction as a spiritual disease, because the drug has replaced God in the addict's life. The 12-step programme was devised by a rabbi to help addicts face their addiction, overcome it and build a new relationship with God. It involves confession, prayer, meditation and reconciliation. Its goal is to restore the person's soul and give them a sense of self-worth through a deeper understanding of their faith. By committing to their beliefs and restoring their faith, they can move forward and once again enjoy the peace and fulfilment of their Jewish lifestyle.

Find out more at: **www.jewishdrugtreatment.com**

Extension activity

Write an article for a Jewish newspaper about the dangers of misusing legal and illegal drugs.

AQA   *Examiner's tip*

When asked to evaluate reasons for and against drug use, remember that Judaism does not object to drug use for medicine or the taking of alcohol in moderation.

Summary

You should now know and understand Jewish attitudes to the use of illegal drugs. Jews believe that illegal drugs harm the person and affect family life and society.

6.10 Jewish schools and yeshivot

Judaism and education

In Judaism, education is considered to be a lifelong process. Studying the Torah is one of the mitzvoth that Jews are expected to keep throughout their lives. Many passages in the Jewish scriptures refer to the importance of teaching and learning in order to develop spiritually and live a correct moral life. Wisdom is seen as a gift from God, as in the case of King Solomon whose sound judgements made him one of the greatest Jewish rulers.

Jewish parents have a responsibility to ensure the education of their children. In addition to attending school, Jewish children also learn about their faith in the home from their parents and they also attend special classes in the synagogue. In these classes, they learn how to read the Torah and observe the religious laws. Boys and girls nearing their Bar/Bat Mitzvah attend special classes to prepare for the ceremony, which celebrates them taking on full responsibility for their religious duties.

A *A Jewish boy reads the Torah at his Bar Mitzvah*

Beliefs and teachings

Teach them the decrees and laws, and show them the way to live and the duties they are to perform.
Exodus 18:20

Teach me your way O Lord, lead me in a straight path because of my oppressors.
Psalm 27:11

Let the wise listen and add to their learning, and let the discerning get guidance.
Proverbs 1:5

God gave Solomon wisdom and very great insight, and a breadth of understanding as measureless as the sand on the seashore.
1 Kings 4:29

Objectives

Understand Jewish attitudes to education and the importance of Jewish schools and yeshivot.

Jewish schools

Throughout the UK, there are a number of Jewish primary and secondary schools. Many of these were established shortly after the end of the Second World War. As the horror of the Holocaust unfolded, many of those who had survived felt a deep need to reaffirm their Jewish faith and practices. In the post war years, a number of Jewish schools opened to provide both secular and religious education for Jewish children. These schools teach the usual curriculum you would expect in any school, for example, maths, English, science and other subjects. However, they also include Jewish studies and make provision for festival observances. Some Jewish secondary schools will also prepare young people for attendance at a **yeshiva** or seminary.

Extension activity

Find out about the preparations that a Jewish boy or girl has to make in order to complete their Bar/Bat Mitzvah. Use the information to write a diary entry for a Jewish child about the ceremony.

Key terms

Yeshiva: a college where the Torah and Talmud are studied.

Yeshivot

A yeshiva (yeshivot is the plural) is the oldest form of Jewish school and offers higher education for young Jewish men, although older men also attend, especially if they wish to train as a rabbi. Women can choose to attend a similar institution called a seminary. A yeshiva focuses upon studying Jewish scriptures such as the Talmud. Those who choose to go to yeshivot are expected to work hard at their studies and they will be continually assessed by oral examinations. Much of the study is done in a process of companionship, where the students work in small groups of similar ability. The idea is that they help each other to learn and only consult their teachers when they need guidance on a point.

B   *Higher education is important for many young Jewish people*

Some of those who attend wish to become rabbis and will have to also take other courses to prepare for this role. Most of those who attend, however, do so because they want to deepen their understanding of their faith. As well as study, the daily routine will also include time for prayer and personal reflection. Many Jewish boys attend a yeshiva between doing their A-levels and starting university and stay for just a year, but others may stay for as long as five years.

Young women who attend a seminary follow a much more structured programme of Jewish studies. The education offered is also broader. As well as Jewish studies, the seminaries also offer courses to prepare for work in professions such as teaching and administration. Women usually attend for up to three years; they will take examinations and be required to produce coursework rather like attending a university.

Research activity

Find out more about the curriculum and ethos of a Jewish secondary school. Write a comparison of how attending this school is different to your own.

If you are at a Jewish school, find out about how a state school which is not a faith school is different to yours.

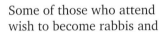
Activities

1   Give two reasons why Judaism teaches that education is important.
2   Explain briefly how Jewish schools help to strengthen the Jewish community.
3   Explain the role of yeshivot and seminaries in Jewish education provision.
4   'Faith schools are not necessary.' What do you think? Explain your opinion.

Discussion activity

'Faith schools cause divisions in society.' Prepare arguments for and against this statement. Hold a class debate and take a vote.

AQA   Examiner's tip

Make sure that you understand the command words used in exam questions. These are instructions such as 'describe', 'outline' and 'explain'.

Summary

You should now know and understand Jewish attitudes to education including the role and purpose of Jewish faith schools and yeshivot.

6

Relationships and lifestyle – summary

For the examination, you should now be able to:

✓ show an understanding of how the Jewish beliefs and law and the principles of commitment and responsibility influence Jewish attitudes to:

– the purpose of Jewish marriage and attitudes to marriage
– reasons why some Jews divorce and the divorce procedure
– attitudes to divorce and remarriage
– attitudes to chastity and sex outside of marriage
– attitudes to homosexuality
– ritual cleansing – the mikveh
– responsibilities of parents and children
– attitudes to alcohol, tobacco and prescribed drugs
– attitudes to illegal drugs
– the role of Jewish schools and yeshivot.

Sample answer

1 Write an answer to the following exam question:

Explain the use of the mikveh by Jewish women. *(5 marks)*

2 Read the following sample answer:

A mikveh is like a big pool. Women go there to immerse themselves when they are ritually unclean. This does not mean that they are dirty. In fact they have a shower before they actually go into the mikveh. In Jewish teachings there are lots of laws called mitzvoth which Jews are expected to keep. Some of these laws describe situations when a person is ritually unclean; this means that they are not pure. When women have a period or after they have had a baby, they are considered to be unclean until they have been to the mikveh. While they are unclean they cannot take part in religious ceremonies or have

sex with their husband and so it is really important for them to go to the mikveh. What they have to do when their period has stopped is go to the mikveh, where they will have a shower and then a helper will say the blessings and then they go down into the pool of water and immerse themselves under the water. When they come up they have washed away all the impurity and they can then continue with their everyday lives. Men don't have to go to the mikveh except on the eve of Yom Kippur which I don't think is very fair when women have to go all the time.

3 With a partner, discuss the sample answer. Do you think there are other things the student could have included in the answer?

4 What mark would you have given this out of five? Look at the mark scheme in the Introduction on page 7 (AO1). What are the reasons for the mark that you have given?

AQA Examination-style questions

1   Look at the photograph below and answer the following questions.

(a)   Describe the roles and responsibilities of parents and children in a Jewish family.   *(6 marks)*

(b)   'Caring for your family is more important than following a religion.' How far do you agree? Give reasons for your answer, showing that you have thought about more than one point of view. Refer to Judaism in your answer.   *(6 marks)*

(c)   Explain Jewish attitudes to the use of illegal drugs. Refer to beliefs and teachings in your answer.   *(6 marks)*

(d)   'All drug use is wrong, except when someone is ill.' Do you agree? Give reasons for your answer, showing that you have thought about more than one point of view. Refer to Judaism in your answer.   *(6 marks)*

 In the exam, there will be a mix of short- and long-answer questions in section A. The exam paper will tell you the number of marks each part of a question is worth. This gives you guidance on how much to write. If only two marks are available your answer does not need to be more than a couple of sentences.

 In section B of the exam, you will be given a choice of two questions each worth 24 marks. Make sure that you read both questions and choose the one that you feel you can write the best answer for. These parts of the questions will need longer answers so you may find it helpful to make a few notes before starting to write your responses.

Glossary

A

Abortion: the deliberate termination (ending) of a pregnancy, usually before the foetus is 24 weeks old.

Adultery: sex outside of marriage, when one partner is married to someone else.

Animal rights: the belief that animals have a dignity just as humans do and should be given care and protection.

Anti-Semitism: prejudice towards Jews.

Artificial insemination: sperm is medically inserted into the vagina to assist pregnancy.

Artificial insemination by donor (AID): a reproductive technology in which semen is collected from an individual, not the husband, and introduced into the female in order to create a baby.

Artificial insemination by husband (AIH): a reproductive technology in which semen is collected from the husband, and introduced into his wife in order to create a baby.

B

Bio-ethics: the study of ethical dilemmas brought on by the progress and use of science and medical technology.

C

Chastity: refraining from sex outside of the married relationship.

Chukim: statutes – laws for which no reason is given.

Community service: work which helps the community – sometimes used as a punishment for offenders.

Compassion: a feeling of pity or sympathy that can lead to caring or help.

Conservation: protecting the natural world.

Contraception: the artificial and chemical methods used to prevent pregnancy taking place.

D

Death penalty: form of punishment in which a prisoner is put to death for crimes committed.

Designer babies: babies whose characteristics may be selected by parents to avoid inherited weaknesses or to choose desired physical features.

Deterrence: to put people off committing crimes. One of the aims of punishment.

Disarmament: the abolition of weapons.

Divorce: legal ending of a marriage.

Divorcee: someone who has been married and divorced.

E

Embryo: fertilised ovum (egg) at about 12–14 days after conception when implanted into the wall of the womb.

Emergency aid: giving needy people short-term aid as a response to a crisis or disaster, e.g. food in times of famine or war.

Environmental conservation: looking after the natural resources of the planet by taking steps to conserve them.

Ethics: the theory relating to morality – the study of what is morally right or wrong.

Euthanasia: inducing a painless death, by agreement and with compassion, to ease suffering. From the Greek meaning 'Good Death'.

F

Fertility treatment: medical procedure that provides help to enable a woman to conceive a child.

Fine: a form of punishment in which an offender pays a sum of money.

Forgiveness: to pardon people for something that they have done wrong. In Biblical times, it is believed that only God could forgive sins.

G

Genetic engineering: when an animal's or human's genes are modified or manipulated.

H

Homosexuality: attraction to a member of the same gender.

Homosexual relationship: a sexual relationship with someone of the same sex.

I

Illegal drugs: drugs whose possession is against the law.

Immortality of the soul: the idea that the soul lives on after the death of the body.

Imprisonment: when a person is put in jail for committing a crime.

In vitro fertilisation (IVF): a procedure in which eggs are removed from a woman's ovaries and fertilised with sperm in a laboratory. The fertilised egg is then replaced into the woman's uterus.

J

Judgement: God deciding about individual deeds, good and bad, and rewarding or punishing.

Justice: bringing about what is right, fair, according to the law or making up for a wrong that has been committed.

K

Ketuvim: the books of writings in the Tenakh.

L

Long-term aid: helping needy people to help themselves by providing the tools, education and funding for projects. This type of aid is given by World Jewish relief.

M

Marriage: a legal union between a man and a woman.

Mikveh: a ritual bath designed for the total immersion of people so that they might be cleansed.

Mishpatim: judgement, laws for which reason is clear.

Mitzvoth: the laws of Judaism.

N

Nevi'im: the books of prophecy in the Tenakh.

Nuclear war: a war in which the participants use nuclear weapons.

P

Pacifism: the belief that violence and war is unnecessary and that there are other ways to resolve disputes.

Pollution: harming the natural world by adding man-made toxins.

Prescribed drugs: drugs which are legal, obtained on written instruction of a doctor.

Protection: to stop the criminal hurting anyone in society. An aim of punishment.

Protest: an action to show disagreement with something, for example government policy.

Punishment: that which is done to people because they have broken the law.

Purpose of life: why a person is alive – what they have to do in their life. The goal of life and the reason for living.

Q

Quality of life: how much a person gets out of their life, a combination of physical and mental factors.

R

Reconciliation: when two people or groups of people who have disagreed or fought with each other make up.

Reformation: punishment with the aim of changing the person's criminal behaviour and making them into a responsible citizen.

Remarriage: getting married again.

Reparation: if criminals commit a crime and are caught, their punishment should make up for the loss that the victim suffered as a result of that crime.

Resurrection: the belief that after death the body remains in the grave until the end of the world, before rising again when God will come to judge.

Retribution: if people do something wrong then they should receive a punishment that is fitting for the crime that they committed. Often referred to as revenge.

Righteousness: behaving in a just and fair way, doing what is considered to be right. 'Justice with compassion' (Rabbi Sacks).

Ritual cleansing: when a person undergoes a purifying ceremony, e.g. a woman bathes in the mikveh at the end of menstruation.

S

Sanctity of life: the belief that life is sacred and belongs to God.

Saviour siblings: babies selected to provide genetic material for seriously ill relatives.

Self-determination: a person's right to choose what happens to them.

Stewardship: the belief that mankind has a responsibility to protect the world God created for them.

Surrogacy: when a woman agrees to become pregnant and deliver a child for a couple.

Surrogate mother: a woman who has a baby for another woman.

T

Ten Commandments: a list of religious and moral rules that were authored by God and given to Moses.

Terrorism: when groups use violence or the threat of violence to achieve their aims, rather than using a democratic process.

Torah: the five books of Moses and the first section of the Tenakh – the law.

Tzedaka: doing righteous acts, giving to charity.

W

World Jewish Relief: British Jewish-run charity to relieve poverty.

Y

Yeshiva: a college where the Torah and Talmud are studied.

Index

A

Aaron 57, 71
Abimelech 21
abortion 18–19, 27
Abraham 8, 71, 115
Adam and Eve 58, 77, 95, 102, 133
adultery 25, 27, 121, 122, 124–5
Africa 38
aid 40, 41
Al Qaeda 66
alcohol 14, 100, 130, 132–3
Amos 34, 55, 102
animal rights 88–9, 92–3
animals, care of 90–1
Annan, Kofi 41
Antarctica 80
Anti-Semitism 60–1
artificial insemination 24
  by donor (AID) 24, 25
  by husband (AIH) 24, 25
Assisi Declarations 84–5
atomic bomb 65
Auschwitz 61, 114

B

Bangladesh 40, 80
Bar and Bat Mitzvah 129, 136
Bet Din 99, 121
bio-ethics 28–9
Brit Milah 129
businesses 36–7, 47

C

Campaign for Nuclear Disarmament (CND) 64–5
candles 21, 50
capital punishment 15, 109, 112–13, 114
carbon dioxide 79, 80
carbon footprint 84, 85
CCTV 101
celibacy 124
charities 42–5, 48–9
chastity 124
Chernobyl 78
Childline 37
chukim 10, 11
circumcision 14
civil disobedience 71
civil divorce 121

civil liberties 101
climate 38
Combatants Letter 69
community service 108–9, 110–11
compassion 20
compensation 102, 114
concentration camps 42, 61, 114
condoms 22, 25
conscience 56, 65, 68, 91, 131
conscription 68
conservation 82–3, 84–5
contraception 22
"Courage to Refuse" 69
courts, civil 99, 108
Covenant 11
creation story 77, 90, 91
credit crunch 46–7
crime 100–1, 135

D

Daniel 31
David, King of Israel 63
death penalty 15, **109**, 112–13, 114
decree nisi 120
deforestation 80–1
demonstrations 69
designer babies 28–9
deterrence 104–5, 106, 107
Deuteronomy 63, 89, 90, 115, 121, 128
  on praising God 16, 50
  on justice 15, 55, 103
disability 18, 19
disarmament 64
discrimination 60
diseases 130
divorce 99, **120–2**
drought 38, 80
drug addicts 100, 135
drugs, illegal 14
drugs, pain-killing 21
duty 9

E

earthquakes 41
Ecclesiastes 54, 95
economies 39
education 136–7
egg (human) 23, 26

Egypt 73
Elisha 130
embryo 26
emergency aid 40, 41
environmental conservation 82–3, 84–5
environmental problems 77, 78
Esau 57
Esther 71, 133
ethics 8
Ethics of the Fathers 55
ethnic cleansing 62
euthanasia 20–1
execution 15, 109, 112–13, 114
Exodus 11, 55, 91, 102, 114
  Ten Commandments 36, 50, 89
extinction of species 80, 81
Ezekiel 106

F

family life 36, 128–9
farming, intensive 91
fasting 73
fertilisation 26
fertility treatment 22, 23, 27
festivals 86–7, 129, 133
fines 108, 110
foetus 19
food laws 91, 99, 127, 129
forgiveness 48, 56–7, **102–3**
fossil fuels 79, 80
Frank, Anne 43, 61
freewill 56, 58, 77, 115
fruit trees 84, 87

G

gay couples 25, 125
Gaza Strip 69, 70
Genesis 22, 30, 54, 57, 91, 125
  creation 18, 76, 77, 94
  man in God's image 114, 131
  marriage 118, 124
  Noah 34, 83, 133
genetic diseases 29
genetic engineering 28–9
genocide 62
Georgia 44–5
Get 121, 122
global warming 38, 78, 80
glossary 140–1
greenhouse effect 78, 79, 80

H

harvest service 86
heaven (Gan Eden) 31
Hebrew language 9, 10, 35
Hebrews 8, 12, 103, 115
hell (Gehinnom) 31
Hiroshima 64, 65
Holocaust 43, 60–2, 105, 114, 136
Holy War 62, 66
homelessness 17, 46
homosexual relationship 124
homosexuality 62, 124, 125
Hosea 13, 103

I

illegal drugs 134–5
illness, terminal 17
immortality of the soul 30, 31
imprisonment 109
in vitro fertilisation (IVF) 26, 27, 29
incest 19, 25, 27
injustice 55, 70, 71
Isaac 8, 57
Isaiah 12, 55
Israel 35, 60, 62, 64–6, 73, 105, 114
Israeli Defence Forces 69

J

Jacob 57
Jeremiah 55, 85
Jerusalem 8
Jesus 103
Job 30, 57, 59
Joshua 12, 62, 71
Judgement 30, 31, 54
judges 108, 114
Judges 21, 133
juries 108, 113
justice 54, 55

K

Kashmir 41
Kashrut, laws of 11, 12
Ketuvim 12, 13
Kings 130, 136
kleptomania 100
Kohen 122–3
Kristallnacht 42, 61

L

Lamentations 59
law codes 56
laws, anti-Jewish 61
laws, unjust 71
legal drugs 130–3
Leviticus 47, 87, 107, 125, 130, 133
Liberal Judaism 22, 46, 47
long-term aid 40

M

Maimonides, Moses 19, 31, 49, 93, 118
Malachi 12, 121, 123
mark scheme 7
marriage 118–19
Masada 68
Masorti Jews 46
medical advances 23, 24, 28
mental problems 110, 113
mercy 55, 71, 102
mercy killing 20–1
Messianic Age 31, 58, 63
Micah 43, 56, 63
Midrash 12, 55, 133
migrash 83, 84
mikveh 119, 126–7
miscarriage 18
Mishnah 36, 114, 115
mishpatim 10, 11
mitzvoth 10, 36, 54–5, 83, 90, 98
Mordechai 71, 133
Moriah, Mount 8
Moses 8, 10, 11, 71
murderers 15, 109, 112, 113

N

natural world 77
Nazis 42, 43, 61, 62, 114
Nevi'im 12–13
next of kin 118
niddah 124, 126, 127
Noah 34, 56, 83, 102, 115, 133
Noahide Code 56
nuclear disarmament 64–5
nuclear war 64
Numbers 67, 71, 84, 94
Nuremburg Laws 61

O

occupied territories 69
Onan 22, 24
Orthodox Judaism 22, 26, 30, 31, 125, 126

P

pacifism 68, 69
Palestinian people 69
parole 106, 109

Passover 129
peace 57, 67, 73
Pe'ah fund 47
peer pressure 100, 134
pilgrimage sites 68
pogroms 60, 61
pollution 78–80, 81
population growth 38
poverty 38–9, 100
pregnancy 18, 19
prejudice 60
prescribed drugs 130
prison 104, 106, 111
prisoners of war 63
promiscuity 124
Promised Land 12, 62
prophets 12, 13, 34, 43, 55, 85
protection 106, 107
protest 69, 70–1, 89, 99
Proverbs 13, 50, 63, 67, 90, 133
  family issues 118, 125, 128
Psalms 15, 57, 59, 63, 79, 136
punishment 98, 102, 104, 105
  impact of 110–111
  types 108–9
Purim 133
purpose of life 16, 54
pushkes 51

Q

quality of life 16, 17

R

Rabbi Abraham ben Moses 85
Rabbi Hillel 36, 57
Rabbi Hirsch 93
Rabbi Jonathan Sacks 34, 35
Rabbi Louis Jacobs 111
Rabbi Shimon ben Gamliel 57
rabbinic interpretations 19, 23
rabbis 19, 47, 99, 114, 119, 124
radiation 64, 78
rainbow 83
rainforests 80–1
Rantzen, Esther 37
rape 19
Rebekah 57
reconciliation 56, 72–3
Reconstructionist Judaism 125
recycling 84
Reform Judaism 22, 30–1, 46, 125
reformation 106, 109
Rehab 71
remarriage 122–3
reoffenders 106, 111
reparation 104, 105
repentance 103

resources 39, 77
responsibility 102
resurrection 30, 31
retribution 106–7
revenge 102, 106–7
reward 115
righteousness 34–5
ritual cleansing 126
ritual impurity 126, 130
Rosh Hashanah 103
Russia 44, 61

S

Sabbath 10, 50, 86, 90, 128–9,
    133
sacrifice 11, 48, 98, 126
Samuel 63, 124
sanctity of life 14–15, 18
Sanhedrin 115
Saudi Arabia 39
saviour siblings 28, 29
science, advances in 23, 28
Second World War 42, 43, 61, 62,
    64
self-determination 20
semen 22, 24, 25
sentencing 108
sex 124
sexuality, human 124–5
Shabbat 10, 50, 86, 90, 128–9,
    133
Shalom 56
Shema 16, 128

Sheol 30–1
sin 73, 125
Sinai 10
slavery 8, 98
smoking 14, 130–1
Sodom and Gomorrah 71, 125
Solomon, King 136
soul 26–7, 30, 31, 54
sperm 22, 23, 24, 25
state law 98–9, 107
stem cell transplant 29
stewardship 76, 77, 94
suffering 58–61
suicide 14, 20, 68, 110
suicide bombings 66
Sukkah 86
Sukkoth 86, 129
surrogacy 26, 27
sustainability 81

T

Talmud 12, 21, 57, 76, 84, 114
technology 77, 93
Ten Commandments 10–11, 21,
    36, 56, 113, 125
Tenakh 10, 12
terrorism 62, 66–7, 113
Tikkun Olam 82
tithes 48, 49
tobacco 130–1
Torah 10, 12, 15, 36, 62, 84, 114
Tu B'Shevat 87
tzedaka 48–9, 81

U

ultrasound photograph 19
United Nations 56, 73

V

vegetarians 91
verdict 108, 112
victims 67, 101, 111
vindication 107

W

war 62–4, 67, 68
    Holy 62, 66
    obligatory 62
    Second World 42, 43, 61, 62,
        64
    against terror 62
weapons, modern 62, 64
wine 133
World Jewish Relief 40, 41, **42**,
    44–5
World Trade Centre attack 66

Y

Yemen 39
Yeshiva 136–7
Yom Kippur 73, 103, 126

Z

Zechariah 57